I MADE IT
THEN I DIDN'T

I MADE IT
THEN I DIDN'T

CHRISTOPHER LOPEZ

Published by Best Seller Publishing®, St. Augustine, FL
Best Seller Publishing® is a registered trademark.
Printed in the United States of America.
ISBN: 978-1-956649-28-4

This publication is designed to provide accurate and authoritative information with regard to the subject matter covered. It is sold with the understanding that the publisher is not engaged in rendering legal, accounting, or other professional advice. If legal advice or other expert assistance is required, the services of a competent professional should be sought. The opinions expressed by the authors in this book are not endorsed by Best Seller Publishing® and are the sole responsibility of the author rendering the opinion.

For more information, please write:
Best Seller Publishing®
53 Marine Street
St. Augustine, FL 32084
or call 1 (626) 765-9750
Visit us online at: www.BestSellerPublishing.org

Contents

About the Author

Christopher is a Professional Entrepreneur. Christopher has opened over 7 businesses in his +14-year career. Christopher's purpose during his tenure was to take advantage of various market-driven opportunities. Christopher is a certified Master Project Manager (MPM) and Accredited Financial Analyst (AFA). Christopher previously held his Series 65 securities license and held a distinction as a Master Financial Planner (MFP). Christopher also has his General Lines – Life, Accident, Health & HMO. Christopher managed above 2 billion USD in assets internationally and domestically working in private fund management. Christopher has work experience in 29 countries, raised over 50mm USD in the private equity space for various businesses, and grossed over 13.0mm in his personal career. Christopher worked in the highly technical industries of: biotechnology, finance, securities, manufacturing, real estate, and residential mortgages. Christopher is a former United States Air Force Veteran. Christopher has a passion for family, competitive sports, fishing, martial arts and advocacy for entrepreneurs. Christopher provides self-help classes for up-and-coming entrepreneurs. Christopher's passion to mentor comes from belief that entrepreneurs need guidance. The world is full of conflicting information about entrepreneur identity. Christopher seeks to clarify the identity of professional entrepreneurs. Christopher resides in Texas and has a beautiful daughter Sofia.

I dedicate this book to the following people who played pivotal roles in my life. A special recognition goes to Crisaly. She was a large portion of my life good, bad, or indifferent. To Don who always was in my corner despite however something looked. To Jeff for loyalty no matter how bad it was. My thanks to Allen for seeing through all the clouds of smoke and believing in me. To Jesse for giving my only trophy. To Leticia for showing me how to love when I never knew how. To both of my mothers Elsie and Veronica. You both loved me the way I needed at different points in my life. Finally, to my daughter Sofia for being the light shining in a sea of darkness. To anyone not mentioned, you are all very important to me. You all know who you are.

Foreword

This isn't a book about failure.

This isn't a book about not making it.

This isn't a book about not achieving my dreams.

So what is this book about? This book is about learning how life works. This is a book that speaks out. This book will directly touch your life. This book is a prospective. It will teach you what it means to live every day without fitting in. What people think you are do not matter. What I am here to tell you isn't theory. I'm not here to tell you about principles. I'm not here to tell you about best practices either. What motivational speakers want you to believe is not in this book. I'm also not here to make you believe you can be the next "Tony Robbins" in motivational speaking. I don't promise you will be the next "Bill Gates" in technology.

I'm here to talk common sense.

I'm here to tell you there are statistics stacked up against you as an entrepreneur. More importantly, I am here to tell you the likelihood of you becoming a billionaire is nil.

My approach is not negative.

I am here to educate you on a person that no one appreciates.

This unappreciated person is successful despite an Instagram following of only 200.

> † **I am here to educate you on what it means to be something that no one appreciates**

This person is the Professional Entrepreneur.

I want you to understand if you are 1) realistic, 2) properly define career, and 3) recognize what an unconventional job looks like you will finally understand success.

I wrote this book because I grossed nearly 13.0mm USD in my career. I have opened and closed businesses you have never heard of. I have a small Instagram following. I do not drive Rolls Royce nor do I wear flashy designer clothing.

I am the 1%...yet you probably have never heard of me.

I will not use names in this book for a reason.

Professional Entrepreneurs do not create brands. Disagree with me?

Read my book and give me a few pages to justify myself. Successful people have patience right?

I wrote this book because by some definitions I am a "nobody". Or at least that's what I was taught to believe. Then I studied. I got a securities license (series 65), became an Accredited Financial Analyst, and saw over 1bn in "unconventional" assets I helped through international audit according to International Financial Reporting Standards (IFRS). I reported a high amount of assets under management at my former practice. Most of my reported assets comprised of a lot of non-traditional stuff. I managed stuff normal people had a hard time classifying as a textbook "security". Most regulators couldn't figure out what I even did (which made things uncomfortable for everyone). I learned during this time. Most people with phenomenal wealth, including high-income earners, thought they were "modestly" successful.

> **Most regulators couldn't figure out what I even did**

I studied some interesting statistics during this time. I learned how much the top 1% of our population earns. I learned how much savings the average US person has. The least appreciated fact (the one showcased by the last government shutdown in 2019 under US President Donald Trump) is **how many people fell apart after missing one (1) paycheck.** These answers will surprise you. More importantly, it will surprise you to learn

I made it then I didn't

something about high income. I will show you how much "money" you need to gross to make more than 9 out of 10 people in the room.

The room I'm talking about is the entire room.

This room includes your high-end grocery stores, your exclusive clubs, and yes…your Galleria Malls.

I also learned the difference between four types of people. I want you to remember them. I will use them a lot in this book.

There is the **Employee**.

There is the **Business Man / Business Woman**.

There is the **Entrepreneur**.

There is the **Professional**.

There is also a cloaked person lurking in the darkness. He or she pretends to be a lot of these. Most of the time they speak well, sound educated, and can get into "situations". Sometimes they are honest. Sometimes they are not. Sometimes they are called scammers. They are people who are at the right place at the right time. They win. They lose too. They scare rule makers because rule makers don't understand them. People you don't understand are sometimes shunned. People in positions of influence are scared of being "wrong". These are the people you must recognize. They are neither good nor bad. They are kind of like the Yin and Yang in Feung Shui. They have both light and darkness. They represent balance to an organization. Often, these people are needed in the beginning. Then these people are typically forgotten when a company they help launch makes it. These people are typically the least appreciated. They are the least useful and then the most useful. With proper use, they are your greatest asset. With improper use, they will be the worst nightmare.

These people are fire.

These people warm you at night but also burn your house down if left unattended. If you don't let the fire burn in the night, you freeze to death too. The world of being an entrepreneur is bitter cold. This world is minus 40 degrees cold.

These people will convince people to believe in "*nothing*". "*Nothing*" is not a scam. Sometimes "*Nothing*" is your first startup. Sometimes "*Nothing*" is Google. Sometimes these people convince people to the detriment of their honest beliefs. No one appreciates them. But if you want to make it you will need them.

I call these people "**Hustlers**".

These people are the key to everything if you need to make something out of nothing.

Do you know how someone broke is still wealthy?

Do you still know how to get equity in an investment when you have no money to invest?

How do you make money without money?

These people have become masters answering these questions. You need to be careful when handling them in your endeavors. I'll explain later. If you are this person, there's a place for you. Just remember your place. Know when to exit. Otherwise, you will get burnt.

This book will contain information no one has ever told you before. I guarantee that

I want you to understand something. This book will not have a traditional ending.

This book will not have a detailed instruction manual. How you make something out of nothing is very fluid. It is reactive. The byproduct depends on the experiment you are running. No two ingredients are the same.

This book will contain information no one has ever told you before. I guarantee that. It will also be practical.

Can you use what I'm writing to make your own instruction manual?

Absolutely.

I will cite real examples and provide facts. I will speak from firsthand experience. I'll talk about recognizing people who will abandon you. I will talk about people who will stick by your side. I'll also talk about people who love you but have no backbone in business (so they roll on you during pressure). I'll also talk about how emotional business can be (something no one oddly likes to talk about).

I'll show you how you can become indicted by simply being associated with someone.

Yes, that last one is scary.

So, pay attention. Learn from some of my mistakes.

Remember there is one lesson I really want you to take away from this book.

The lesson is simple.

"Don't be something you're not and don't assume if you don't ask questions it will be okay".

I will not teach you how to build a great *brand*. That's what **Businessmen** and **Businesswomen** do. I will teach you about a hidden class of people no one talks about.

These people you most likely know. Everyone under appreciates these people. <u>But these people you don't recognize (and most likely know) are your statistical anomaly.</u>

An interesting statistic I want you to pay attention to is something from the US Small Business Profile of SBA Office of Advocacy (2018). There are 24,155 small business employments (individuals) who have a 100% total private employment figure in "Industries not classified". Who do you think these people are?

> **I will teach you about a hidden class of people no one talks about.**

These people are Professional Entrepreneurs. These Professional Entrepreneurs are the classification with the highest probability you will become if you make money the way I detail in this book. Women also have a sizable part of this classification. I am not very main stream. I will not neglect women like so many others neglected by main stream in this citation. So pay attention. Don't feel like you're a failure if you are a **Professional Entrepreneur**. The sad thing is these types of people earn more money than 90% of the country. **And no one talks about them or celebrates them.**

Most that I have spoken to think they are "just getting by". Imagine that. **Someone who earns more than 9 out of 10 people doesn't even know they are successful.**

If you are one I am here to recognize you. I am here to tell you to be proud of yourself. If you do not understand what I am talking about listen up. This book comes from my 13 years as a "**Professional Entrepreneur**" who started out as nothing but a *"Hustler"*. I rubbed two pieces of air together to pull a gold bar out of thin air (literally). No one appreciated me. But I have learned to appreciate myself.

An important concept to grasp is value and worth are two different things. Do not let your worth be determined by other stakeholders.

Intrinsic worth is how someone defines and measures themselves.

Value is marketplace need for what a person offers. Someone can have extreme worth and relatively low value.

People once thought diamonds were hard rocks and discarded them. Imagine being the person who thought a diamond held no value?

The diamond's value changed but the stone's worth was always the same. Remember that.

I wrote this book because someone needs to tell people like us that we do have "value". Most importantly, I was compelled to tell people like us that we are "successful" by conventional standards.

Averaging over 100k a year consistently for 10 years is successful.

If you're new to what I am talking about I will show you a niche to get into. What you will get into has better odds than what conventional business statistics show you. The odds you will build a multi-million dollar business to become the next Bill Gates are less than 1%. That's a fact. The chance you will get a market share and stay in business over 2 years is less than 10%. The statistics according to some lead trend researchers below to see what I'm talking about.

According to a 2013 Forbes Article by Eric Wagner 80% of entrepreneurs starting a business fail within the first 18 months. (Forbes)

According to data researched by Statistic Brain, 50% of startups fail after operating for four years. (Statistic Brain)

According to information published by Tutsplus, 66% of small businesses will fail within 10 years. (Tutsplus)

In 2012 Small Business Trends found that 50% of small businesses fail after five years. (Small Business Trends)

The Wasp Bar Code researched that 3 out of 10 new companies "fail to survive" for more than 24 months. (Wasp Barcode)

Credit Donkey published claims after conducting research that only 33% percent of startups reach their 10 year anniversary. (Credit Donkey)

The leading paper USA Today in 2017 found that only 1 out of 5 new businesses survive past their first year of operation. (USA Today)

Fundivo found that fewer than 50% of businesses survive more than 5 years. (Fundivo)

What I will show you in this book has at least a 50/50 chance of earning you some money. Before you get on coin flip probability admit it's better than conventional startup statistics you just read. What is amazing if you learn what I detail in this book (if you have what's needed), you can earn money within 6 – 9 months. Sound crazy? Not really. It's the same thing I've done time and time again (at least 4 times by my current count).

So, let's focus on something that is at least as likely as a coin toss. Stop believing in something that most likely won't happen.

I'm not being negative.

I'm being factual.

I want to show you how to even the odds. I want to show you how to "win". I want to show you how to "recognize" success. Others don't make a big deal of your success because you're not on Instagram. Who cares if you're not on Instagram? I sure enough don't. Some of the wealthiest people I know have zero social media presence. This is not to say Instagram or social media is irrelevant. I am not a specialist in social media. There are legitimate ways to earn money this way. The important lesson I will teach you is how to determine who you are. The worst thing in the world is for an **Employee** to be an **Entrepreneur** or an **Entrepreneur** to confuse them-self with a **Businessman / Businesswoman. That is where the degree of failure comes in**. Trust me it happened to me.

The point is there are identities with earning money. Each core identity has its specialty. Each specialty has its category. Each category has a subcategory.

Just because your crossover doesn't succeed does not mean you didn't win. You won until you tried to be something you weren't. Go back to what works. That's what I did.

> **I want to show you how to "recognize" success when others don't make a big deal.**

Don't get down on yourself. Don't say you failed. Let me show you how to make over 100,000 per year regardless of your business' longevity. Let me show you how to earn more than 9 out of 10 people regardless of whether or not anyone knows your *brand*. More importantly, let me show you how to make money with "zero" social media presence or notoriety.

A **Professional Entrepreneur** is a *profession*. It either pays money or it doesn't. If you're making over 100,000 a year who says you don't have a good career?

Do I have you convinced?

Lessons You Learn on Your Own

EVERY GOOD BOOK starts with a story. Each book starts with some monumental feat that shapes the author's character. So I want to ask you something. It's simple and straight forward.

Nature or Nurture?

Do you understand the question?

For those that may not be familiar with what I'm saying, what I'm asking is what type of belief do you ascribe to? There are two well-debated ideas on what each offers.

Some say the nurture aspect is important because it shapes who we are. The environment you are born into influences everything. Your environment influences your behavior. Your choices, attitudes, values, ethics, and ultimately your love / hate come from environment.

> **The environment you are born into influences everything.**

Then, there are those that argue your DNA embeds everything. Who you are is who you always were meant to be. These proponents of nature say our environment doesn't matter. After all, we hear stories all the time. Two siblings brought up in the same environment turn out completely different.

How does that happen?

Some say it is because of nurture.

An interesting concept into Nature & Nurture is published in a Peer-Reviewed Paper called "Contemporary Research on Parenting, The Case for Nature & Nurture" (Collings, Maccoby, Steinberg, Hetherington & Bornstein – American Psychologist, 55(2), 218-232). In this paper, the authors state "The heredity and environment of an organism can be completely separated only in analytic thinking, for in actual nature such separation would lead to instant death of the organism, even though the philosopher making the analysis might himself survive."

In laymen terms. I know.

This statement says if you remove both there is no possibility of life.

I'm saying the same thing to you. Stop talking about where you come from or what "pedigree" you are. What you do with yourself and your environment has everything to do with who you become.

You can become a failure of a rich family, an anomaly of a poor immigrant, or just achieve more than your parents did.

You can interchange each other role as well.

This is what I learned in my childhood.

I am a Puerto Rican and Dominican heritage American. I love the fact I am American. I've been to about 29 countries in my life as a professional (I might have left off a few). I saw many cultures. When I was a child my biological father (I have a dad whom I call "Pops" and I'll get to that later) was

What you do with yourself and your environment has everything to do with who you become

in the Air Force. So we moved around a lot. Stable for a child? Not by any conventional definition. The experiences that occurred in my "Nurture" influenced my "Nature". These experiences created situations that built the person I became. As an adult, I learned it was up to me to interpret my experiences. How an adult interprets their childhood experiences defines what type of person he or she becomes.

It isn't the other way around.

In your childhood I'm sure you had some dramatic event happen. When it happened you might have been upset, scared, victimized, filled with joy, or some other emotion. *When you were a child strong emotional trauma drove a reactive behavior.* The reactive behavior became a habit. After habit consistently applied to your life it became part of your subconscious identity.

Now as an adult you must choose.

The choice is how you want to define yourself.

Do you want to be ruled by some childhood trauma which tells you who you are?

Or

Do you want to wake up to the trauma and choose to be who you are?

You must dig deep. You must decide. Are you ruled by childish instinct? Or do you want to decide what to do with your trauma and become what you should be?

As a child, my biological father embarrassed my mother. While we lived in a small island he produced a child out of wedlock. During those days there was no internet, social media, or even cell phones. You had to write letters and choose to physically see someone. You could live two separate lives 100 miles away. My father blatantly disregarded considerations of my mother. As a child I interpreted my father's actions incorrectly. Empathy was taught to me as irrelevant. When he left my mother with four small children to start a new family, his actions said: "families can be changed". His actions told me your children's feelings are not what are important in your life. By all definitions, he said, "follow your own pursuits". He told my mother he wanted to pursue being a business owner at any cost. The woman he chose was a woman of wealth. My father saw the other woman as his way of making it. My father thought he could use her, make money, and then come back to my mother (at least that was one side of the story). He convinced her through manipulation he was something he wasn't. Anyone can fall for a con if their emotions are invested. My mother & father were friends since childhood. My father assumed she would understand. Both were born in the 1950's when stuff like this happened. My entire family line was a byproduct of my Grandfather's "mistress".

My Nurture was not so encouraging.

My biological parents did not nurture me to adopt any of the following characteristics:

Empathy
Compassion
Fairness
Loyalty

Justice

Dedication

What my father taught me to do was, "follow my dreams at all costs". My father taught me to be selfish in pursuit of monetary success.

Have you ever heard this saying before?

"The *Ends* justify the *Means* no matter the cost."

Yeah, that is what my father taught me. So how do you think I behaved as a child into an adult? I got one big character trait from my childhood trauma. I became "extreme". What do I mean by "extreme"? I would do "anything" to accomplish my goal. Literally, I would do anything. I became "stubborn" because of these Nurture events. I became so stubborn I gained some interesting positive characteristics. These characteristics were:

Hard Working

Diligent

Focused

Self Motivating

Creative

How I reacted to my childhood events embedded unique aspects in me. Instead of longing for a normal family, I was very amenable to the introduction of strangers into my life. At my seventh grade awards, I won an award called "Mr. Congeniality". The award symbolized most people found me likeable. I found out the most effective way to make a friend was by doing a nice, surprising thing which only their closest friends would do. I would act like this even if I only knew the person a few days. My actions were perceived

> Instead of longing for a normal family, I was very amenable to introduction of strangers into my life.

as thoughtful. As a child, it could be something simple. In one instance I volunteered to hang around to ensure a friend didn't get jumped in a fist fight. Once I knew someone liked Papa John's pizza, so I voluntarily purchased the person a slice without them asking for it. I did all these things without anyone soliciting me. It's not every day someone walks up and says to you, "I don't like that person either. I'll fight them with you." To an adult it sounds childish. To a child it sounds like "Wow". What made these child-hood events more impactful was I was not even friends with the people. I did things like this as a child to earn loyalty and friendship. When people asked me why I did it, I answered with something about their character. I would describe how I liked something about them.

This all ties into earning money. Trust me. Just keep going on with the lessons.

Being thoughtful usually doesn't cost much. Being tenacious and having no fear costs a lot. I always played a big stakes game when I was young.

I learned if I was willing to risk myself in challenging circumstances and explain why I did it in a way which singled out a positive character trait it created loyalty. Inspiring loyalty was how I received what I wanted.

There is no bigger compliment than coming to someone's aid because of genuine appreciation for who they are.

Trust me on that.

It's how I landed my first love in middle school. I wanted her so I once pushed someone on the ground when felt her butt without permission. I wasn't her boyfriend at that moment. When she asked why I did it I told her all the great things I admired about her. Needless to say, she became my first childhood sweetheart. I wrote her letters about things that no one else noticed. She loved me (well as much as a child could back then) for it.

My sense of thoughtfulness came at the cost of self-interest. Some could say that was selfish. In some sense maybe it was. What I wanted was companionship, friendship, and not being alone. Ironically I overcame rejection because I was rejected by my father. Fear of rejection is why most people never succeed. People say using people is wrong. I always asked myself why was that a bad thing? I never understood why a person wouldn't want to be useful growing up. I learned from my father using people was the only way to be.

The point of this chapter is not to "use" people.

You must open your eyes to see how you were "Nurtured".

The surprising revelation is I didn't know I was doing any of this. I simply did. That's kind of the point to this chapter.

To become a "**Professional Entrepreneur**," you have to start with understanding one huge concept.

People.

The point of this chapter is people.

You must be a master of people. Understand why they do what they do. Understand their motivations, their desires, and most importantly why they make decisions. You can only do this once you answer the most fundamental question there is. That question is

"Why do you do what you do?"

There's no answer I can give you. Everyone is different. Everyone has their own nurture and their own nature. Dig down and get to the place that allows you to get that concept. I stopped drinking from the age of 21 to 25 (more or less). I even stopped being intimate with women from about 22 to 24ish. I found the answer in answering the question below.

"Why do I do what I do?"

Once I realized who I was, I was able to excel. I was looking for myself. I lacked a lot of experience. The most important thing I didn't lack was self-insight and self reflection.

Substantial Growth is done in isolation.

Substantial Growth is done when you are not in a romantic situation.

Substantial Growth is done when you do not surround yourself with people.

Self-insight allowed me to have excellent communication because I became comfortable with who I was.

Where did I get a good foundation for communication? By trying to make my childhood sweetheart fall in love with me (let's emphasize "try" a lot). Don't forget about those love letters.

I listen to understand not to respond. It's not a competition on proving who is right and who is wrong.

Let's summarize what you need to take away from this.

I need you to focus on understanding all your tendencies.

Try to understand why you must skip a car to get to a red light which makes you wait anyways. Understand why you don't enjoy cutting your nails in public. All the little things that seem irrelevant are the things you have to understand. All these small events go back to a certain place in time in your life that told you, "Hey you're alive. Here's this event. What you want to do with it?"

Why have I spent so much time on this?

I've found in every successful deal I've been part of something peculiar was consistently overlooked. People with money are "people". They are not some god descended pillar of a community. They are not imposing super heroes. They are people with unique behaviors. And like anything people with money "appreciate" when someone takes a **genuine interest** in who they are. Don't fake interest. Anyone with some wit can tell a phony. People in business must be keen on discerning the difference. If your take away from this chapter is to understand yourself so you can understand others...you're missing the point.

> **I've found in every successful deal I've been part of something peculiar was consistently overlooked.**

Understand yourself to care about yourself.

Then understand people **to care about other people**.

True feelings for another person's well-being are real. And trust me, people feel it. If you're a sociopath or someone who lacks this ability, I have a rude awakening for you. You won't be successful at being an entrepreneur. You will not be a person who makes their profession a **Professional Entrepreneur**.

Remember, we are talking about a *profession*. We are not talking about amassing a wealth that rivals the next multi-millionaire. We are talking about finding out a way to earn money with people who are completely different. These types of people are different from 99% of the population. To work in this world, you must understand it.

This world is nothing more than people. This world consists of a distinct peer group. Like the cool kids in school when you were young. If you wanted to hang out with them you had to figure them out.

Remember, you can't figure anything out until you figure yourself out.

That's where it all starts and ends.

Think about your nature. Then define your nurture. Once you do that move on to the next chapter.

Natural Questions That Define Who You Are

AT SOME POINT in a person's life, a moment comes when the person asks questions. Questions at these points cause us to act. These actions seem insignificant as older adults. As adolescents, children, or young adults these moments can be very monumental.

When I was in the fifth grade, I enjoyed being my age. I did all the things young boys did during the 1990s. I played with action figures, sticks, imaginary items created from my video games and anything else that used my imagination.

Then I arrived at middle school.

My peers didn't do the things I did at all.

My new peers played basketball, chased girls, acted like new rap artists (this was the mid and early 90's during gangster rap) and demeaned my otherwise creative behavior (as childish).

What do you think I did?

I stopped doing what I did in an instant.

We went from middle class to very poor. My mother survived off government assistance

I wanted to fit in with a new group of children. Before I came to middle school in Orlando Florida I still had some semblance of a family. My family structure changed when I moved with my biological mother (as it was after the divorce of my biological father). We went from middle class to very poor. My mother survived off government assistance, part-time government work (as a cashier at the military base commissary), and various other side things she could do to get us what we needed. The area they forced us move to was poorer than what we were previously accustomed to. As a consequence, I ended up in middle school at Howard Middle School. At one point I remember tooting foolish records. I was once proud to be from the school with the most fights in the State of Florida (to showcase my hardened nature).

Howard Middle School received the majority of its student population (at the time) from what they classified as "extreme lower income" areas. In walking distance from my old middle school is a street called Orange Blossom Trail. To this day people still know it as a street you can solicit prostitution. Today the city is taking a much more aggressive stance to root it out. Back then crackdowns were pretty much nonexistent (think 1995 time frame). Because of Howard Middle School's location, young African Americans dominated the student population at that time. Most of the student population came from crime-ridden areas. Latino population trailed second. Caucasians were an "extreme" minority. Asians comprised a whopping total of maybe 10 students (not exact but I remember they all literally sat at one table during lunch). Definitely not diverse.

If you completely abandon who you are inside, you will lose yourself.

SO I asked myself, "How can I make these people like me?" Once I answered this question, I did everything I could do to change. I wanted to fit in. I modified my dress, adjusted the way I spoke, and took up hobbies others did.

Throughout this process, I "never" lost my identity. That's important. If you completely abandon who you are inside, you will lose yourself. More importantly, you will develop self-hate. That's not good. My negative by product was getting my self-worth from the value others said I had to them. This is also a bad trap which is easy to fall into. Unfortunately, I did not figure this out until after I divorced my ex-wife. I derived my self-worth opinion from her value. When she devalued me because of a mistake I made I became unhappy. This unhappiness led to depression. When I couldn't do anything to change her mind, I became hopeless. I ended up bankrupt because of this and walked away from my marriage.

She thought I quit.

I was just miserable and had some growing up to do.

Avoid the negative by product your worth is determined by another person's value.

Your usefulness and their desire to involve you in their life is determined by your value. Value has nothing to do with your intrinsic worth. Remember diamonds were once discarded rocks.

The real purpose of this narration is to illustrate a point. I realized I needed to change my behavior to be accepted by certain groups. Some call this "Conformity". Conformity is a great character trait for ***"Hustlers"***.

To some extent *"Entrepreneurs"* need Conformity. When I apply this to *Entrepreneurs,* I mean it in the context of associating with your desired peers (not being unoriginal in business or not being innovative).

A nonconforming approach applied to your target peer group will create difficulty developing a social relationship with the group. To work your way up in an organization, a business, or become associated in a transaction you have to possess what's called "likability". Likability is garnished by conforming to positive expectations.

> Conformity is a great character trait for *"Hustlers"*

Evolved Likability is "Charisma".

A good entrepreneur realizes the most important thing they offer is his or her presence. The ability to command a room full of people is an important aspect to presence. Commanding a room allows you into opportunity.

I am not talking about public speaking.

I'll give you a subtle example I applied in my life.

In 2019 I held an insurance license for life and health. I was solicited to join a team. I figured since I held the license I might as well put it to use. I was invited to an interview to discuss being part of this insurance agent team. I saw nearly 200 people had shown up. Everyone was vying for the opportunity to be part of the program. I immediately realized this was a tryout. Even though I was solicited I was not picked. I had to do subtle things to create focus on me. I had to accomplish this goal if I was to make an impression. I could not do it by standing up and shouting "Hey Everyone Pay Attention to Me!"

If you want to be the center of attention, you cannot look like you want to be. You must not appear forceful in your approach. Instead, do peculiar things which attract attention and curiosity.

This is what I learned to do when I was young (in middle school).

When I walked up to the front desk the first thing I did was smile. I then gazed into the receptionist's eyes. Many people look, some people stare, others don't pay attention and look somewhere else.

I gazed.

Gazing is not the same as lusting or showing someone you're interested. It is a distinct look that shows a hint of "admiration".

What do you think the receptionist did?

She locked eyes with me looked away and double took me. My first signature win. *Attention.*

She asked who I was here to see. My second opportunity to create an opportunity.

Choice of words.

Many people answer, "I'm here to see Mike", or worse "I don't know", or "I spoke to Jim" or "I had a 230 appointment". All clear, concise routine responses.

I answered, "I'm here to see the person who created this awesome presence."

She looked at me like "*What?*"

See! What I said wasn't a compliment about the office. What I said wasn't a compliment about her looks. What I said wasn't a compliment of something specific.

My compliment was a good thing for sure, but it was abnormal. I was different with my words. My compliment forced her to ask herself, "What is he talking about?"

She then confirmed I had an appointment. I answered routinely. I'll get to how this stood out in a bit.

I proceeded to the room, sat down, and took out my clipboard. I started answering the questions on the clip board. I took time to glance around the room while I filled out the form. I observed how people dressed. I studied their movements. I wanted to see who my competition was.

I would watch people walk up and down the hallways (we had a glass wall which permitted us to see through to the hallways). Everyone was wearing expensive Versace shoes, gold watches, and other outward signs of money. It was at this moment I decided to take out my Mont Blanc pen. I placed my Mont Blanc in my vest pocket clearly visible to everyone (I'll get to why this was important later). People would come in and announce names. People would stand and shake hands. I noticed the first thing most interviewees did was make small talk with their prospective interviewers. Some people would walk down the hallway only to return a few minutes later. Then they would abruptly go home. I picked up on what these short time intervals were quickly. What the interviewers were doing to the prospects (i.e. people like me) was removing people who didn't belong.

My third opportunity.

Create a presence.

They called my name.

A younger guy named Joe came up. Joe shook my hand. He signaled to follow him so I did. While we were walking, he asked how I was doing. How do you think I responded? Think I said "good" or "great"?

Try again.

I looked around and noticed the features of the office. They had trophies. Literally the office was displaying glass trophies. They looked like super bowl trophies. Do you think I asked "What are those?" *Try again (lol)*.

I recognized the trophies were an important feature of this office. The trophies expressed a highly valued ethic. That ethic was *"Competitiveness"*. I realized I was in a place where interviewers had to see as many people as possible. They required high volume to see if prospects were people who would perform under pressure. The first comment I said to Joe was to illicit reaction. When he asked how I was doing I said, "I'm anxious because I'm looking for a place where my drive to win can be expressed."

Bingo

His eyes lit up.

Joe said that was great. Joe said that this was exactly the culture that the organization provided. Joe asked me about my background. I told him with as few words as possible what I did. I emphasized things that mattered to the organization. I emphasized things like 100mm in accounts within 18 months at my former practice, 100% incentive-based compensation

† Joe asked me about my background. I told him with as few words as possible what I did.

models. I compared my activities to the number 1 producing firm in Houston at Merrill Lynch. I beat out individual account originations for the year by value.

What these actions are illustrating is an important feature of a **Professional Entrepreneur**. The feature is "Identify what not to talk about". Don't talk about things people do not care about. When someone asks you about yourself they are really asking:

"What is it about you that would make me want to continue to be around you?"

Do not give responses in a lot of words. People don't track long monologues. Make it concise (not short there's a difference). Ever heard of the expression "what is your gut feeling"? Your job is to give someone a good "gut" feeling about you. It is impossible for someone to trust you after one conversation. What you can do *in one conversation is make an impression*. That's what I learned from "Conforming". So let's play this theory out.

When Joe and I concluded with our short walk down the hallway do you know what he did? He handed me his personal card. Joe said "If you don't get a call back give me a call."

See Joe recognized in a short walk I was someone worth talking to again. But Joe is not the goal I was hoping for. Joe was part of a chessboard I was setting up.

Let's continue.

When I reached our destination, I was in an auditorium style room. In the hallway was a Vince Lombardi Mural. The mural was a dedication to being "Number 1". It's a famous speech Vince Lombardi gave about what it takes to be number 1.

A short excerpt goes as follows: "Winning is not a sometime thing; it's an all the time thing. You don't win once in a while; you don't do things right once in a while; you do them right all the time. Winning is a habit. Unfortunately, so is losing…" (Vince Lombardi).

> **Winning is not a sometime thing; it's an all the time thing…Winning is a habit… Unfortunately so is losing.**

I immediately knew this was not a place for mediocrity. More important this was not a place to come if you believed you could just coast. These people were looking for top performers. It was obvious. There was another interesting concept to the mural's speech.

The other part of the excerpt went as follows: "…And in truth, I've never known a man worth his salt who in the long run, deep down in his heart, didn't appreciate the grind, the discipline. There is something in good men that really yearns for discipline and the harsh reality of head-to-head combat…" (Vince Lombardi)

This speech embodied something about the organization. The Lombardi mural was important because it literally took up an entire hallway. What's more was the Lombardi mural was on full display for a room full of over 200 people. The thing that got me the most was…no one paid attention to it. They were too busy trying to talk about themselves or worse their unrelated experience. I overheard so many replies to people talking about themselves like "Well that's great for then but what we do is…"

Do you see the issue?

No one paid attention. These people wanted *Conformity*.

We live in a society that promotes individualism. That's great. Be you. The issue is sometimes people don't want a chief. They want an indian. You can't say, "Hey make me part of your team on my own terms." That's not going to happen. Since no one really attempted to conform to their culture it left a vacuum. I filled this vacuum with *subtle charisma*.

You can't say, "Hey make me part of your team on my own terms." That's not going to happen.

The first thing I did to give subtle charisma was walk to the front. I sat right next to the podium. Everyone else filled out in the middle and the back. I sat in a place where I could be recognized. While everyone else sat at attention I noticed no one was taking notes. So I pulled a notepad out (amazing how many people don't bring note pads).

I was the only person in the room to take out a notepad and use it. I started blatantly using it in front of the speakers. They noticed. I angled the notepad where they could see how organized it was too (bullet points, starts, underlines, et cetera).

Guess what?

The speakers noticed everything.

Imagine that. They are supposed to be public speaking. Instead of paying attention to the entire public room they were focused on me.

Subtle Charisma works wonders.

About 5 times throughout the presentation 3 separate speakers asked for my name. They also used me as an example in communicating a point.

I also had an expensive pen (a Mont Blanc) I constantly angled in a way the speaker could see (remember my observation from earlier). I did this because everyone talked about high earning potentials for selected candidates. People earning as much as they were saying (300-400k per year) usually pick up a Mont Blanc at one point or another. I needed them to know that I was accustomed to earning money. I was trying to tell them, "You don't need to teach me how to do it. I already do."

At the end the speakers asked us to give a short few sentences about ourselves. The speakers also asked us what we took away from the presentation.

Bingo the final opportunity.

I want you to understand something. It's something that comes from one of my favorite authors Anthony Robbins (yes I'm citing him for psychology purposes). In one of Tony's books, he talks about how people primarily remember two moments in an interpersonal interaction. People remember the first thing you do and the last thing you do (not the in between stuff). Those are the most important moments according to Anthony Robbins. I agree.

This was the last moment.

People stood up and talked about everything under the sun. It ranged from mundane culture, to pay, to working with people. People talked about almost anything you could think of. Some talked about how they didn't want to pay for licensing (No call back material I'm sure). What people did not do is something important I believe needs to happen when making first impressions. People exhibited no unique body language when delivering closing remarks. People would stand up, hands at the side (or behind them), and then either slouch or stand up straight.

It was pretty much that uneventful.

I think the dust bunny dancing in the air vent had more presence than a lot of these people.

I recognized two things these people value. I needed to communicate these values when it was my turn.

These people valued "drive".
These people valued "performance".

I stood chest out. Rather than having my hands to the side I waived (something no one else did) and then I said the following

"I don't know if anyone has ever been a champion before. But in this room and this hallway you can tell this place breeds champions. If it doesn't make sense to you that's okay but that's the most important thing I've taken away. And it's exciting."

As I said that I brought both my hands up as if I was carrying something (palms up). I then grasped them like Conan the barbarian.

I cannot understate my point. These actions inspired each major director, producer, general agent, and anyone else who was paying attention to light up. It's like a fire came on.

I sat down and said thank you. I spoke for maybe 30 seconds. Others spoke for up to 5 minutes before being told to "keep it short". From that point on everyone kept staring at me. I intently listened to everyone else smiling in a relaxed manner. I purposefully did not get up until everyone else spoke. I listened to everyone. The speakers told us we could go turn in our pamphlet to HR after talking. My decision to wait was important. Many got up and walked out. By remaining I showed leadership I valued "team". I wanted leadership to see my actions.

When I finally left, leadership pulled me to the side. They thanked me personally. When I walked out to the front lobby, I handed the pamphlet to the receptionist who used my name on departure. She said, "Bye Christopher" and winked at me. I smiled at her. I replied, "I'm glad you remembered my name." She smiled. I learned later why they conducted the group interview. There were

I recognized key features about "other" people's values. This was not about how I found a place with <u>my own values</u>.

approximately 3700 people applying for the position, 200 selected for a group interview (after multiple phone interviews which I had too), and only 50 were called back. But their receptionist remembered my name.

Guess when they called me back?

In three hours.

I came in for the interview the next day. Do you know who they asked me to pair with? I paired with the lead regional agent. This regional agent was the right hand-man to the owner. You would never guess what he showed me. Even I was caught off guard by what I saw. He showed me my resume with the word written "Stud" at the top.

Listen to the point I'm trying to communicate.
It's not about being praised or getting an ego boost.
I recognized key features about "other" people's values.
I showed empathy for others' values.

This story is not about how I found a place with <u>my own values</u>. This isn't my gloat about getting a good job. I paid attention to other people (not myself). I "Conformed" with the culture to receive attention. <u>More important I "Conformed" in an exceptional way</u>. After "*conforming*" I knew I must possess "Charisma". Charisma would help me control the room (through interesting and peculiar behaviors). Finally, it was paramont to not seem arrogant, cocky, or talk about meaningless things (to my peers).

Most people believe being themselves is enough.

Being just yourself is not enough for greatness.

Being yourself is enough for mediocrity.

Be more than yourself.

I'm not saying to be fake. I am not saying to lose yourself. I am not saying to be something you are not. **Be all the qualities you are** <u>that</u> <u>matter to the people you are talking to</u>. **Professional Entrepreneurs** recognize the most important thing they can do is fit in to the peer group they are trying to do business with.

Hustlers are renowned for doing this. You see *Hustlers* with Caucasian real estate developers in their mid 50's by day and hanging out with early 20-year-olds in the hip hop entertainment industry by night. Hustlers understand relatability, communication, and empathy exceptionally well. Exclusively promote qualities you

† Exclusively promote qualities you possess, that each prospect wants to see, and you will transact many types of entrepreneurial deals.

possess, that each prospect wants to see, and you will transact many types of entrepreneurial deals.

I have more substantial business situations to discuss. Each one is raised as it specifically relates to a relevant lesson. This is not an autobiography. The difference between me and my other competition is distinct. I will show you "how" <u>applied theory</u> yields "real" results.

You can then judge the "results" for your own benefit.

In this book, you will not hear about grandiose tails. You will not hear of my phenomenal accomplishments for no particular reason. That is called "Grand Standing". Grand Standing is not the point of this book; however, I admit sometimes you need "Grand Standing". When is it needed? An example of when to use Grand Standing is when a person you want to listen has an ego the size of the Earth. Most people with egos listen to respond and not to understand.

Egotistical people typically listen for breaks in your conversation to interrupt you, reiterate their point or argue their evidence is better than yours.

Definitely, Grand-standing is not one of my favorite characteristics to promote in an effort to conform. With huge egos, you need Grand-Standing occasionally to grab the charisma needed for the big ego to pay attention to common sense (literally).

At certain points in our lives, we come across times that force us to ask questions about how we can "fit in". For me, it started with wanting to fit into a culture. I was completely foreign to the new group of kids I encountered in middle school. My desire to fit in was not a unique trait. We all desire to fit in. We all desire to be accepted. Learn to express the character traits required to get what

> **With huge egos, you need Grand-Standing occasionally to grab the charisma needed for the big ego to pay attention**

you desire. Most people desire to be part of something they think they can't be a part of. You can be a part of anything if you put your mind to it. You must remember conforming is part of your job as a **Professional Entrepreneur**. I never understood people who said, "I can't work with people in that industry." To me this is a closed minded person. Learn how to conform during working hours. Learn how to use conformity to build social relationships. Use conformity so people like the traits you present.

Once you have approval, you can amplify those traits to exude charisma. Once your traits are exuded take control of the room. Become what everyone desires. Once you have interest <u>promote your own objectives</u>. Once you are what people desire, your desires become what they desire.

See how that works?

Now people want what you want. Your agenda (your true self) comes full circle.

The question you need to ask is, "How can I fit in but still retain my true identity?"

Never lose sight of who you are.

When you lose sight of what you are (even me) you will lose in your endeavors. I lost when I decided to be more than a **Professional Entrepreneur.** I crossed into being a **Businessman**. I'm not a **Businessman**. I lost big trying to be something I wasn't.

Once I went back to being a **Professional Entrepreneur** I started winning again. I'll get to that later too.

Learning Past Your Own Oblivion

DO YOU REMEMBER the first time your parents talked to you about how much something cost? Do you remember being put in a position when you were first required to earn money? Do you remember what it was first like to realize one thousand dollars was hard to earn?

I did.

I remember when I was a senior in high school. I had to come to grips with reality. I would graduate in a year, so I needed to learn about adulthood. I was recovering from a football injury I received and had time to reflect. During the fall of 2003 I was ahead of my class. I only had three classes left to graduate. I finished school a full semester early (I was done with class in December of 2003). Usually football consumed my full attention and I thought of nothing else. Once I injured myself, I realized I was going to miss the entire season. I had a lot of time to think. One of my older brothers was living in the garage at the time. My brother was about 8 years ahead of me. He had experience venturing out on his own and providing for himself. So I often went into his room all the time. I would talk with him about my future. During this time it shocked me to learn my parent's mortgage was 1,081 USD per month.

When I was 17 years old I began to think, "How can I make one thousand dollars a month and still live like I do now?"

The thought was intimidating at that age.

I found most jobs in the area for my age paid 5.15 – 7.00 USD an hour. I realized if I worked 40 hours every week for a month I wouldn't even take home 1,000 USD.

I was petrified at the thought a hard-working person couldn't afford a decent lifestyle.

So I did the natural thing. I thought about college. I spoke to my brother in the garage and asked him what his thoughts were about college.

Not much luck there.

He had a bachelor's degree which earned him a garage living.

He showed me anything not sales had the expectation of a whopping 35-45,000 per year starting off. A 4-year non-technical bachelor's degree with no experience would earn you limited income back then. I couldn't even make as much as my mother was making back then. My mother had some college but primarily worked her way up as a government employee in the commissary. The better option was to just get a job, work your way up to a management position if I was aspiring to make 35-45,000 per year. At least in that position I wouldn't carry on student debt.

This was like having very large wool uncovered from my eyes. I had no way to replicate my current lifestyle (which wasn't overly lavish) through hard work alone. In football they taught me hard-work was the key to success. In the real world, it appeared hard work mattered but not enough to get you paid. That is still true to this day. I know a lot of hard-working people that don't make over 50,000 per year.

> In the real world, it appeared hard work mattered but not enough to get you paid well.

I asked my brother for any information he had about improving my situation. My brother gave me a book. It was the greatest first read I ever read.

The book he gave me was "Creating Wealth" by Robert Allen.

Creating Wealth was a real estate book from the 1980's. Robert Allen talked about earning money during the S&L crisis. During the 1980's interest rates on mortgages were as high as 20% per annum.

Imagine that.

We complain about 5% interest rates on mortgages. People in the 1980's were taking out 15-22% interest loans. Back then it was uncommon to exceed 10 years on a mortgage. Now there is a 50 year mortgage product being promoted (go figure).

This book opened my eyes. I saw it was possible to make 10,000 on a single deal! I realized other people's money (OPM) would get me into real estate. Hard money lenders and alternative investors were available to me as well. This new concept of real estate was exciting to me. I never planned on making 1mm USD through real estate. I only wanted to earn enough to live like my parents. That was always my goal. If I could make 40-50,000 per year doing real estate this was the answer I was searching for. Learning past your own oblivion is an important concept.

> **Learning past your own oblivion is an important concept.**

When I was 17 I learned past my oblivion. I did this with real estate concepts I never heard before.

This book will do something similar to you. I will show you some things you never heard before.

Society often tells us what we should or should not do. The baby boomer generation promoted the mantra, "Go to school, get a college degree, and work 20 years at a top firm".

This mantra is obsolete.

People have been under the oblivion that markets do not exist. People have been under the oblivion markets cannot change countries. Countries have cycles just like economic cycles. Baby boomers lived in a unique age. Europe had its entire infrastructure destroyed (from World War II), the US Government had large silver stores (Any coin from before 1964 had a silver content for .40 - .90 pure. That's why a burger cost a nickel), and we were the only developed country with an intact manufacturing infrastructure (we were one of the few major industrial countries to not receive bombing in the country). The US was also not as technically advanced as it is today. Much of the work was "manual" (i.e. not automated by machines). When you combine these unique characteristics with a significantly smaller working population, you have the perfect recipe for,

"Abundant jobs where employers compete in a limited employee space by offering unheard of benefits."

The point of this section is to point out society does not operate under any previous generation premise. You must remove economic "oblivions" taught by your parents. Our parents are not at fault for teaching us what they did. For the first time in history society changed with unheard of speeed. Our parents' instincts to teach what they did was not wrong. Many generations operated by a standard for centuries. Some generations operated by a status quo for thousands of years. We are the first generation to change faster than our biology. Our instincts are struggling to catch up with change engineered by technology. Our cycle of manual processes shifted overseas fast. Business flocked to cheaper cost of labor. Only in today's technological

The point of this section is to point out society does not operate under any previous generation premise.

world does it make sense to make something 5,000 miles away and ship it here; instead of making it in your backyard with no shipping. Logically it makes no sense to have this arrangement. Yet technology has made this illogical concept true. Our population is rapidly increasing in an age of automation. Automation means new jobs are not created to cover increasing population.

There will never again be the number of benefits offered in the past in today's current market. Current employers are not required by the market to deliver lifelong pensions.

Having a job is enough.

In my opinion, the future will have a very strong push toward Universal Basic Income (UBI). UBI will implement itself in government policy to offset the void between earnings and jobs. Ray Kurzweil, a well-respected Futurist Predictor, predicts UBI by 2030. Mr. Kurzeil is well known for predicting many modern-day technologies. He has done so with a plus 75% accuracy since the 1990's. Stockton, California recently ran an experimental UBI program. The idea was to give people $6,000 a year to see how it would affect low-income residents. The program in Stockton was pioneered by Mayor Tubbs. In the paper UNDP China Office a Policy Option for China beyond 2020, by Agi Veres UBI was discussed at great length. According to Agi Veres, the appeal of UBI is partly linked to major social-economic trends. These trends are being observed worldwide. The trends include constant levels of poverty and growing inequality.

These trends have signaled a prediction. I predict there will be few ways to earn significant sums of money in the future. I predict large sums of money will only come if one fits into categories I discuss in this book. At some point in the 2040's, I believe hourly based wages will become obsolete. I believe during the 2040's, UBI will elimi- nate high earnings for the **Employee** category. If these predictions happen, a path for the **Professional** will emerge as a must if a person desires to earn sig- nificant money.

> I believe during the 2040's, UBI will eliminate high earnings for the **Employee** category.

A **Professional Entrepreneur** is required to have strong fundamental knowledge of market con- ditions. As a **Professional Entrepreneur,** you must understand markets create rifts of opportunities. These opportunities sur- face from three circumstances:

1. Disorganization
2. Emerging Concepts (Technologies & Industries)
3. Personal Reasons

Each one of these three circumstances are your entry into a market (it is not important which one as they all have similar features for oppor- tunities). I need you to open your eyes. Just like I did as a 17 year old, I need your eyes to recognize these three circumstances. These three circum- stances are what will create your opportunities.

As a **Professional Entrepreneur,** you will often find yourself as a "One Person Band". A "One Person Band" means you do not have the resources or credibility of large corporations. You will not have the same staying power as large corporations. For instance, you will not be able to weather a 24-month negative cash flow. The statistics you learned about business are correct. Most businesses will not positive cash flow their first 12 months. Most businesses lose money. Most businesses lose money for a long time. As a **Professional Entrepreneur,** you are in a profession to earn money without being "employed".

> As a **Professional Entrepreneur,** you will always be kind of "One Person Band".

This means you must find special situations. These special situations allow your aptitude for recognizing a deal to shine. Remember you are working in an environment occupied by businesses as well. The businesses are like the Greek gods. This means you are like the Greek Titan. Titans walked amongst the Greek gods. The Titans were resourceful, powerful, and had great talent. The Titans did not persist in the realm of the Greek gods, however. As a Titan you must be careful to not overstep. As a Titan, you must take advantage of what most Greek gods (large corporations) are ignoring. The metaphoric Greek gods (large corporations) ignore the three circumstances I mentioned above regularly.

In these circumstances, you have all the advantage. Generally, none of the big corporations are participating in these areas. It is also important to note these opportunities typically only exist in a special space. I call this space a "Middle Space".

What's a Middle Space?

A Middle Space is where a person has put enough money into a company to prove a concept (usually 150,000 – 500,000). The Middle Space Company has sales (albeit not impressive numbers) but the Middle Space Company has yet to reach a mature point. A mature point would be when the company's product/service is completely dominant or the company accounts for at least a 5% market share. In other words, the people that operate these businesses need help they cannot afford. They are also not "Start-Ups". Start-ups are their own animal. Start-ups require a completely different skill set to launch. Let's not confuse the two.

Here is the other part that some of you may not like to hear.

You don't get paid upfront for these situations. **You have to be performance based**. What typically turns people on is the compensation is extremely high and highly excessive. If performance-based compensation turns you off you cannot be a **Professional Entrepreneur**. Remember, people always pay for what they don't know. People also pay very high for "maybe". As a **Professional Entrepreneur** you must be okay with "maybe". Maybe you get paid or maybe you don't. Middle Space **Businessmen / Businesswomen** pay handsomely to attract the following: 1) resources for additional business, 2) money for expansion, or 3) money for payment of your professional expertise. Undercapitalized businesses

> If performance-based compensation turns you off you cannot be a **Professional Entrepreneur**.

will always surrender money for your efforts post-closing. Many do so at huge multiples (most of the time in excess of ten times the going rate). Sometimes your efforts only take 3 months. Sometimes your efforts take 6 months. The most your efforts should take are 9 months. Very seldom will you see your efforts pay off in anything short of 60 days. If you have been doing something for longer than 9 months and are not at least into 60,000 for the year – you probably are in the wrong situation. You need to get out and count that endeavor as a "loss".

Professional Entrepreneurs have losses sometimes.

The flexibility of being a **Professional Entrepreneur** means you are there for the "*opportunity*", not the "*business*". Remember that.

I'll explain more about that later.

Let's go over the primary circumstances in detail to discuss how these opportunities come up. Let's start with the easiest one.

Personal Reasons

Personal reasons are about as self-explanatory as you can get. The reason an opportunity surfaces is indicated in the title. The personal reason a person has for presenting you an offer will vary.

For instance, I have a long time friend that is from the East. He will only work with me during certain times. There is a concept called Feung Shui in Hong Kong (and also mainland China). This concept centers on annual cycles, elements and certain celestial signs. I am a Wood-based Ox with a strong affinity to fire. I consider my efforts unlucky when I venture into metal-based endeavors (Because metal cuts wood). If this does not make any sense to you, that's okay. This book is not about Feung Shui. This is an illustration of how I approached him during a wealth accumulation year (for him) so he considered it the "Right Time". He felt it might result in an "Opportunity" being presented to me (provided it agreed with my charts). So, he went into a deal with me for this reason.

> **Personal reasons are about as self-explanatory as you can get. The reason an opportunity surfaces is indicated in the title.**

This is an example of extreme Personal Reason. Not everyone will chart the stars to do a deal with you. None the less, this is an example of a Personal Reason and how I became involved in a multi-million-dollar deal.

These situations come up because of interpersonal development and relationships. These items never surface if someone is not a genuine friend. Remember, I mentioned the concept of being genuine?

Let me give you an example of how a genuine action for expressing concern can forge a relationship. The relationship I formed would end up being a close friend of mine. He is still a good friend to this day. I had a relationship with a third party business broker in 2009. I met my friend through the business broker. The business broker had originally called me up to see if I would assist in a complex transaction. I declined. I informed the business broker I had my own transactions in the space. The business broker asked me if he could introduce me to my friend to garnish some credibility. He thought he might even do a transaction with me. I agreed. I made a good impression but the business broker wanted to go another direction. I would end up saving my soon to be friend from participating in a bad transaction. The bad transaction was uncovered to be a fraud. In this fraud he could have lost 10mm Euros. Yikes. That would have hurt. No wonder why he became my friend! I do not like inconsistencies in people. Persistent inconsistency typically means a person is dishonest. That is what this business broker and his group were. I'll explain how. I became involved in this deal after a long period of silence because the the business broker wasn't getting anywhere with my friend. The business broker was stonewalled. My soon to be friend remembered the impression I gave him on our few calls. My soon to be friend informed the business broker he would only move forward if I had an endorsing opinion concerning the deal.

He had never met someone that would make that decision. That's the only reason we became friends.

The business broker called me up and made me an offer. The offer was 1mm to an attorney escrow account of my choosing. Once my soon to be friend from the east signed the deal, the business broker would authorize the release of the 1mm to my account. This generous offer surprised me. I was caught off guard. I asked him what he needed me to do. The business broker said he needed me to review a contract and assure my soon to be friend everything was exactly as represented. I saw this as odd. Why not use an attorney? I agreed to review the contract. What do you think I saw?

Inconsistency.

I spotted inconsistencies in the busines broker's contract I did not like. The words he said did not match up with what he wrote on paper. More important he found ways to legally capitalize words to mislead a reader. I did not like that.

I withheld my endorsement.

The business broker called me up with his attorney.

I turned down a 1mm cash offer during a time I was hurting financially.

Do you know why?

Character.

Integrity.

Morals.

Honor.

Verbally the business broker was saying the exact opposite of his contract. The contract called for something my friend specifically did not want to do. The business broker and the issuing institution were clever. These parties hid a misleading term in a technical banking definition that lacked definition in the recitals section. As a result, my friend from the east didn't catch it. My friend's attorney did not catch it either. I did. For this reason, I thought the guy was conducting fraud. When I told my soon to be friend what was happening, including the offer given to me, he was floored. He had never met someone that would make that decision. That's the only reason

When approaching a Personal Reason never have an agenda. Listen.

we became friends. As a result I saved him from a very compromising position. A few years later anyone who did business with the group lost all their money. The venture was a complete belly up bankruptcy. I have never made any money with my friend from the east but we've remained close through the years. We've come close to doing a few deals but we have not fully gone the distance. Maybe we will at some point in the future.

The only way a situation with this type of person will come up with you is if the person learns to trust who you are. More importantly you must be given opportunities. The opportunities must prove that it pays for the person to remain committed to your friendship throughout the years.

Money comes and goes but your reputation echoes for eternity.

Remember the previous chapter?

Learn how to interact with people and genuinely care for them. This is the only way to take advantage of Personal Reasons.

Having a true connection with someone will create a sense of confidence in you. If you are around during the right moment an opportunity can surface.

When approaching a Personal Reason never have an agenda. Listen. Don't offer to be part of the deal if you bring no value.

Listen to understand.

Do not listen to respond.

A seasoned business person will value someone who doesn't look like a vulture. The person may even insist you become a part of it despite having no skill set for the deal! I have watched ill qualified people elevated to high positions based solely off "trust". If a person brings a situation up don't refuse to offer help. Sometimes a person brings up a situation to you to see if you want to help. Offer your help if you think you can bring value. Don't stand idle and pass on the opportunity because a person didn't directly ask for your involvement.

People don't talk about things for no reason.

Here's an example of another opportunity. A person is a personal trainer. The person works out all the time at your gym. The person has the characteristics of a self-starter. You always have conversations with them and share common goals in exercising. Then you ask "What type of stuff do you do outside of the gym?" You end up finding that the person runs an outside boot camp. You ask if the person needs help to get attendees. The person answers yes. You ask what it would look like if you refer people to come to their events that pay. The person offers you 25% of everything they make. Now you get paid for promoting a person's services. This is a real person I know. This person is one of my dear friends.

Personal reasons come in varying reasons and sizes.

I'll give you another spur of the moment Personal Reason. This one came through another close friend. He asked me to be a trustee for an estate. This person was an attorney as well. We did numerous trusts formation deals together. I originated people who would become law firm clients. Since I gave my attorney friend's firm so many clients, sometimes I would help him on drafting the documents. I would point things out, solicit his feedback, and then finalize it with my attorney friend's final approval. The work we did together made him comfortable with my decision processes. I must have on average brought him 30-40,000 per year in client retainers from 2008 to 2018. Most of the clients centered on business structuring. They always paid me separately. I would combine my work with his legal work so he could always make money too. In this way my attorney friend knew I would always look out for him. Although it was never a direct marketing relationship my attorney friend recognized the work we did together. He always appreciated me for recognizing his talents. We became very close friends. We became close to the points where we were (and still are) brothers. Then he asked me one day to watch over his entire estate on some private stock deal he did if it paid off.

Imagine that? I didn't even ask him for it. He offered me an opportunity to make money for a personal reason.

He trusted me and I appreciated the vote of confidence. So I accepted. There are more qualified people than me. That is not the point. The point is I am competent *enough*.

This opportunity was not presented because I was the most competent attorney or trustee. I received this opportunity because he recognized something he could do with me that he couldn't do with others...what do you think that was?

I'll give you a hint. It's in the word "Trustee". Emphasis added on *Trust*-ee .

He trusted me. I appreciated the vote of confidence. So I accepted. There are more qualified people than me. That is not the point. The point is I am competent *enough*. My attorney friend looked for a reason to involve me. The company is (fingers crossed for its success) on its way to go IPO via Nasdaq. If the company works out the way it is suppose to, there will be a large ticket.

I received stock in that company for another reason. I'll briefly detail that as an "Emerging Concept".

Emerging Concepts

An Emerging Concept is something that takes root before anyone finds out about it. An Emerging Concept is like a seed that will blossom into the next great forest. The issue with Emerging Concepts is they are the most difficult to spot.

I have argued the ability to recognize a deficiency in a market as a talent. Not everyone can see something coming before it comes. There are tell tale signs but the signs are not obvious.

I'll give you a real live example. I spotted something which turned into something great.

In 2015 I met the head of cancer research at a reputable university. The person was a well-respected scientist. The person had little business experience but created scientific research that was amazing. One of their treatments struck a chord with me personally. The treatment had application to someone close in my family. I met this person through a mutual associate that felt we needed to get together. I did not seek this person out and was asked specifically by someone to help him (reputation and respect are important). The scientist showcased numerous grant awards from the US Department of Defense, National Institute for Health and even showcased a deal that was being done with one of the richest businessmen in the pharmaceutical industry. The man he was working with was Patrick Soon Shing. These were all impressive things. I was really taken back by the level of his accomplishments. His mentor was a man that might have created more patents in his space than anyone else (like ever). I was so amazed by their accomplishments I was curious. I wondered how much money these scientists made doing all this incredible work. In subtle ways I pried. You know what I found out?

They didn't get paid much.

Here I was looking at all these different technologies going to market, transacting multimillion-dollar deals, going public (and a host of other things) and the creators of all this wealth were being stuck in a lab.

They were essentially being paid little bonuses and being told "good boy keep making us millions. Take your 120 to 200k per year and be happy."

At this moment I recognized the "Emerging Concept". A unique opportunity existed when you were doing research at a university. If you would pay for the patents, pay for the pre-clinical work to discover the sequencing (off the site of the university), and then bring it back into the lab to be developed – you could do so with government funds / grants **and still own the Intellectual Property**.

† **Remember I had no formal training in science or biology.**

In a straightforward sentence, "If you go somewhere else and pay for something to be designed. You own it. The school will take it back because they need grants for valuable research. Valuable research means the school keeps getting government money. Qualifying for grants means the universities will develop your stuff at no cost so they can get indirect cost money to pad their pockets."

Genius.

This was my Emerging Concept.

Remember, I had no formal training in science or biology. I recognized the agriculture industry was losing large swaths of crops (in Florida all our orange groves were dying to canker). Numerous articles were available stating crop loss was amounting into the 100's of billions per year. No one had a solution.

Then I saw a "Middle Space" opportunity. A man who appeared to have all the answers didn't have the money to properly promote himself or his team's talent. He couldn't afford to give me any money (save a small sum of 5,000). He needed me to go find the money.

I found the money alright. I will chronicle this story in detail in my later chapters. My story will illustrate a lot of valuable lessons.

You don't have to be an expert in a market to figure out where it lacks innovation. Nor do you have to be formally educated in something to understand the likelihood of it working. I admit education is important. So don't discard education as if it doesn't matter. Recognizing Emerging Concepts requires experience. Sometimes you only find experience in previous opportunities that "failed".

Sometimes you only find experience in previous opportunities that "failed".

That's true.

It's for this reason I put the hardest one after the easiest one. Now let's finish with one that's in the middle.

Disorganization

Disorganization occurs when an opportunity surfaces where people are making money but no central authority exists. An example of this is the crypto market. No one is regulating the market. There is no major player. In a disorganized market anyone who has the ability, drive, and desire to do something can do it. There is no great licensing barrier. If a disorganized market has a license involved, there are typically loopholes allowing unlicensed people to make money.

Some people call disorganized markets "True Free Markets".

Disorganization is a Professional Entrepreneur's dream.

Disorganization is a place where you will find our knife in the dark… the *Hustler*.

Every good entrepreneur I know got their first start with 1) a *Hustler* partner or 2) as a *Hustler* themselves in the <u>Disorganized Space</u>.

I was a *Hustler* before anything.

I still am.

Let me give you a great example of Disorganization. This example is how I saw my first success. In 2006 I noticed that banks gave out stated income stated asset loans. Banks allowed good credit score persons to "state" their income; provided they had enough of a down payment. If the down payment was high enough the banks believed it showcased substantial equity stakes. The banks believed substantial equity stakes proved people would not walk away from mortgages. As a way to entice high down payments banks allowed you to "write" your income without "verifying" it with the bank (yes banks allowed that at one time). There was a time when no one formally verified an applicant's income to support their mortgage payment. All banks cared about were a large down payment (usually 10-20%). That's how abundant loan money was back in 2006. The banks figured responsible people with good credit scores would not abundantly commit fraud or mismanage their financial position.

I used this information for the right reasons.

There were obviously some people who took advantage (the movie "Big Short" comes to mind).

I found long established business owners who had money but took all their income as Self-Employed earnings. A Self-Employed person has no consistent income. They do not have pay-stubs. You must project what a Self-Employed person might make based on their past. They are a bit harder to underwrite. A Self-Employed person compensated their income uncertainty with

Me and my brother sold 250mm USD worth of new construction homes up & down Florida.

sizable down payments. This is what the loans were originally meant for. Unfortunately, without quality control banks allowed McDonald's workers to own 3 houses.

Back to my use of this market. My Self-Employed businessowners would put down money to buy multiple properties. Their income fluctuated by year so we would average it out. Remember there are no salaries with owning your own business. You will not have any W2 income as a business owner. You must state your income. Again, this was the "purpose" of stated loans when they first came out. They did not design stated loans for what you saw in the "Big Short". The "Big Short" was why so many mortgage brokers went to jail or lost their licensing. Stated loan programs were supposed to be products offered to business owners. Stated loans were not for your next-door neighbor who worked at Wal-Mart because they had a 750 beacon score.

I opened my Real Estate Company and Mortgage Company to take advantage of this market in 2007. I did this with two of my brothers and a great mentor. Glenn Wesley Turner (GWT) was an awesome man who was a huge part of my success. If you don't know the name look him up. He has a book called, "The Sharecropper who turned $1,000 into $100,000,000".

He was such a big reason why I found success. He passed away sadly this past year. I loved the man. He will forever be remembered by me.

I encourage you all to take some of his philosophies and lessons. Watch one of his speeches. He was the original motivational speaker. Everyone else is just a spin off from him.

GWT mentored Anthony Robbins. True stuff.

I was lucky to call him my father-in-law and him to call me son (We were related through my brother's former marriage to his daughter).

In order to get referrals from GWT approved my team averaged the last three tax years of their income and wrote it down. We categorized them as business owners and collected their tax returns to compile financial forms. We submitted them according to the guidelines given by our lenders.

Once we submitted them approvals came in.

I was so young back then.

Imagine grossing 500,000 dollars in a single month before 22 years old?

This type of performance made me fantasize about how many houses I could buy and sell.

This fantasy led me to a book by Gene Burns & Dolf De Roos. The book is "52 Homes in 52 weeks". The book is a good read if you want to see aggressive entrepreneurial tactics at work. Gene and Dolf's performance was my goal and marker to pass. Me and my brother sold 250mm USD worth of new construction homes up and down Florida. We did not have licenses but employed a licensed mortgage broker, licensed real estate broker and a real estate attorney. Laws were different back then. Non licensed people could own licensed entities. This allowed us to enter the market. We focused on bringing investors to buy real estate in large quantities in Florida. Given the regulators didn't have a progressive stance (no housing collapse had occurred), and that no one believed you could get wealthy buying and selling multiple homes (it was a new concept back then) we capitalized.

Today you see all types of house flipping shows. House flipping was like a secret back in the early 2000's. Also Youtube and social media were not a thing in the early 2000's. You had to read to see success. Most people don't read for knowledge. So it was easy for us to beat out our competition. I always read. Reading is a character trait of nearly every single successful person.

Exceptions do exist.

Just remember Exceptions are not the rule.

Possible and probable are two different things. Just because something is possible doesn't mean it's probable. It's possible a meteor will hit us tomorrow. It's probably not a very good probability though; so I would not plan my day around it.

It's not very probable a person who says they don't read will be successful.

When I first got into entrepreneurial deals to earn money it was 2006. In 2006 it was the time of the "American Dream". Back then the American Dream was, "Every American will own a house and get a good job out of college".

Credit restrictions eased, cheap money became available, and newly innovated products called Adjustable Mortgages came out like no one's business. It was an aggressive time.

When I first got into entrepreneurial deals to earn money it was 2006.

Mortgage Brokers could have unlicensed Loan Officers too. As long as the Mortgage Broker reviewed and signed the deal anyone could originate a loan. Now it's different. Another interesting fact was we didn't need to be licensed to own a real estate brokerage firm. There was also no requirement to obtain a license to own a mortgage brokerage firm. They also allowed owners to prepare closing documents for mortgage broker review. They allowed owners to handle direct negotiations with potential customers (if a licensed broker was present). As long as the signature to close a deal was from a licensed person you were golden.

Regulators allowed developers to put all things on something called a HUD Statement in the pre-collapse market.

A HUD Statement is something that is a formal closing document. The HUD Statement fully discloses who gets paid for what. The rule was

"As long as it's on the HUD it's a legitimate closing fee."

We worked by gathering large pools of accredited investors. Our accredited investors were people who wanted to purchase houses with money down and great credit scores. The key part to our success was we filled a need unavailable at the time. We provided the opportunity to accredited investors qualified by assets

> **The key part to our success was we filled a need unavailable at the time.**

only. Our clientele base was usually older people. These clientele had large cash deposits but limited employment income (sometimes none at all). All our clientele were very successful people. The majority had liquid net worth values in excess of 1mm USD. Our people held virtually no debt. They had amassed their fortunes from a lifetime of success. Now retired they had personal companies which were often 20 years old. Our investors were perfect candidates to invest into real estate. There was no strategy at the time for purchasing bulk purchases while preserving market value. There were issues that surrounded developers in a boom market. One of the issues was how to preserve the value of the house while selling multiple houses to one person. Sometimes developers needed to get into a later phase of development to meet milestones or adhere to lender covenants. Sometimes the developers simply mismanaged cash flow and realized they couldn't make the next interest payment. So rather than default on some covenant or payment the developers would look to get rid of a lot of inventory fast. The strategy for package sales typically resulted in low ball offers. Most bulk purchases in real estate are just people asking for things at a discount. Selling houses for less than market value is like death to a developer. Developers needed to convert their construction loan to a permanent loan.

Converting a construction loan to a permanent loan is a huge advantage to developers. It drastically reduces the interest rate when a developer gets rid of a construction loan. The carrying costs of a construction loan can eat up a developer's profit.

Once 4 to 5 people were under contract, I knew we could move anywhere from 10 to 20 properties at a time. Back in those days, they allowed you to buy a primary home, a second home, and up to two investment properties (depending on how much you put down on each one). If someone was willing to go subprime (i.e. take a high-interest loan) we might do three investment properties. After we got preliminary approvals we would negotiate bulk purchases with developers. Developers were eager to do this to get their next draw. Finishing a phase of construction allowed them to finish their phase of development. Finishing the development meant a lower interest rate. Sometimes finishing the phase meant they could get a restart on their no payment period.

These are all good things for a developer.

The trick was structuring it where the developer still profited but didn't hurt the market value of the house.

A lot of times a developer will take less profit, but the developer needs to understand how the transaction will not affect the value of the property.

We were masters at this.

The title company considered our fee a "Marketing Distribution" under a Joint Venture Partnership. We would sign a Joint Venture Agreement with the Developer. This Joint Venture Agreement would allow distribution from the title company after the bank funded the loan. The title company would distribute our money once closing was settled. A title company is a company that handles real estate closings (if you are wondering). We were always paid after closing not during closing. This was an important aspect of our deal. Since at closing all the money was technically going to the Developer (with a marketing fee distribution going post closing) the property was deemed to be sold at full price.

We preserved the value of the property, sold the house for its appraised value, cleared a hefty fee and saved the developer a lot of money. We saved the developer money by converting the construction loan to a permanent loan faster. Sometimes we saved the developer from default.

You can imagine how happy these developers were to do busines with us.

Before 2009 regulators allowed unlicensed people to be on a closing statement (HUD Statement). The bank would fund a closing statement that contained unlicensed people; provided they were related to a licensed party.

The market was different then.

Those days are gone.

The point I'm making is that there was a lot of Disorganization back then.

There are a lot of similarities going on now (as of 2021) in the crypto market. This I think is a good market to pay attention to. Apply the characteristics of the housing market to the crypto market and I'm sure you will identify an opportunity. I have personally found several opportunities which yielded me significant earnings this year.

Unfortunately, crypto investing is not a topic of this book.

<u>Disorganization is where</u> **Professional Entrepreneurs** thrive because there is seldom a well-capitalized business in the market. The market in Disorganization is full of one man / woman shows. A disorganized market also has people with little to no reputation. Competing in a disorganized field is where a **Professional Entrepreneur** can shine. In a disorganized field the **Professional Entrepreneur** typically only has to beat out one girl or guy.

Remember, the condition of society was different in the early 2000's. There was no such thing as "Running infomercials". There was no mass culture was trying to teach people how to make millions in real estate before 2010. There was also no side hustle culture in the early 2000's. Most people just wanted a decent paying job. Decent paying jobs were generally available. Cost of living was not astronomical.

It was possible in 2000 to live in New York, Miami or Los Angeles by yourself on a server's pay. Today living in these cities with that type of work is incomprehensible.

Today there is a huge gap between wages, cost of living and housing prices.

Today's condition of society is not like it was during the early 2000's.

People didn't realize you could become wealthy through real estate. People before 2010 didn't realize a credit score would result in the ownership of 5 homes. The only reference before 2010 was Donald Trump. The only books on making money in real estate were in a small self-help section back then. Typically, these books were tucked in a corner out of sight. The real estate tycoon Donald Trump dominated any real estate section (keep in mind he already came from a millionaire family). Today there is an entire real estate section in a book store.

You can also see commercials on ESPN. These commercials tell you about the next millionaire seminar. The commercials come on right in between a sports game. Everyone states you can make money in real estate.

I saw it as I was working out the gym the other day.

Today it is a normal thing and yesterday it was a pipe dream.

I call today's entrepreneurial real estate market a "**Saturated Market**".

Professional Entrepreneurs avoid Saturated Markets like the plague.

Disorganization is how I grossed my first 1mm USD. As a matter of fact, my brother and I grossed about 5.24mm USD from 2006 to 2009. It was a good time for us. Then we learned about "Market Cycles". I was too young to recognize booms and busts. Unfortunately, I was caught up in the bust. My assumption, "Anyone with 100,000 in savings, a 700 credit score, a 20-year-old business, and was willing to pre pay a mortgage for 6 months could always buy a house" was dead wrong.

> **Disorganization is how I grossed my first 1mm USD.**

The Realization of a Hustler's Importance

One key component to my success was recognizing the fact I needed a *Hustler*. I was by all definition a *Hustler*. I was hardly an *Entrepreneur*. I was too young to have experience. So I did what all *Hustlers* do. I hustled a *Hustler* to become partners with me. My brother and I met someone. We will just call him Hustler C. Hustler C was a true Hustler. This guy was a former CPA who

> **I was by all definition a *Hustler*. I was hardly an *Entrepreneur***

knew his way around. He was in his mid 40's. This guy was a real smooth talker. Hustler C was the type of person that would talk his mom off a ledge even though she knew there was nothing but cement below.

Hustler C was a person we met at a networking event. He was into buying real estate as well. He met with us and we exchanged information. What Hustler C saw in us was what my brother had. My brother was once married to a very famous person's daughter. This relationship allowed us to have a makeshift investor base that could be solicited. When Hustler C met with my brother's former father-in-law he saw opportunity. Hustler C agreed to be the credible one and work with us as partners to attract new people. We made a partnership with Hustler C that was literally worth his time. You may hear me refer to something called a "Cost Benefit Analysis" from time to time.

That's important.

Time is the most valuable asset.

Always make something worth your time and another person's time.

Be measurable, concise and SIMPLE. People who make money don't like hearing speeches. They like hearing plans of action that are workable and easy to follow.

Don't be over complicated.

Say your plan in 4 or 5 sentences at maximum.

Wait for a question to decide if you should talk more.

Read body language to see if someone has interest.

We had at least 10 people to use for our strategy before Hustler C would contribute. With a lack of authority on who would provide these services to developers, we had ample opportunity. Hustler C could pose as the former CPA who had liquidation resources to older developers. The younger *Hustlers* then came in to negotiate the deals and bring forth investors.

> *Hustlers* enhance the opportunity. *Hustlers* make others believe in something else. That something else was two brothers in their early 20's.

The partnership worked very well.

My brother and I met with one person after another. We had to learn to manage this guy. He did such a great job with his "5 Pillars Speech".

If we left him un-kept he would probably have closed the deals himself and paid himself without us (remember the fire analogy at the beginning). It was important we were always with him when pen went to pad. It was the speech about Hustler C's philosophy on business and his charisma that always captivated people in our meetings. So we used him. He was smart too; not a dumb person by any means (I mean he was a CPA at one time). He used us too. He knew he could get at least 10 people out of us based on our family ties. He was well read, well-spoken but when you got down to the brass tacks of it all; this guy had no business. He had no legacy and nothing to show for all his talent. If you asked him to show you three years tax returns and "source" the income – you would have maybe fifteen 1099s from people you never heard of. That didn't make him illegitimate; it made him a *Hustler*.

Hustlers have no brand.
Hustlers only have themselves.
Hustlers are nothing more than good words with incredible presence.
Hustlers typically have one or two credible verifiable facts about them.
(Think the fact he was a CPA but remember the fact he was a CPA.)

Hustlers enhance the opportunity. *Hustlers* make others believe in something else. That something else was two brothers in their early 20's. We had no track record but we had a lot of ambition.

A previous personal hustle was making people invest over 1mm USD into a guy and his team who didn't even have a company. Before me they were nothing more than science teachers at a school not known for producing anything (I mean commercially they weren't on a Forbes list). I don't say that to demean my former team. They did incredible work. What my former team's research accomplished was amazing. The truth was they were nobodies. They were not a nobody because I said so. I am labeling them nobody because nobody knew who they were outside their circle. The definition of nobody (in business) is a person who is nobody to the public. That does not imply their lives are not worth something. That does not mean the people were not special to someone.

I'm not an animal.

I'm just phrasing things in a business context. To a large extent, I am nobody. That doesn't mean that I get down about it. I'm just realistic enough to recognize it (I.E. I don't have an ego).

Do you see now why **Hustlers** can be your close friend?

The Closing out of a Disorganization Market

It was at the end of the 2010 market when my opportunity in Disorganization started to unwind. With the huge foreclosure numbers occurring and people being desperate the regulators were pressured to blame someone. Regulators started vigorously going after anyone who did a "stated" loan. Regulators wanted to blame the people who made the boom happen. Blaming people who propped up the success was the easiest option. With any industry, you will have fraud. Regulation will not prevent it. It will just discourage it. The real drawback that comes with regulation is the departure of **Professional Entrepreneurs**.

I had no negative repercussions from this "overregulation" because our business was "clean". Unfortunately, I would not come out clean on my second go around. It really does matter who you associate with. I'll touch on that later. I made a choice to move on from my real estate market when the most we could hope for was a 1% commission after twelve months of on-time payments by a new borrower.

The "Big Short" chronicled the end of the real estate market very well. It is about 90% accurate. It's scary when Hollywood accurately characterizes a real life thing.

Regulators turn Disorganized Opportunistic markets into **Saturated Markets** meant for the everyday consumer. No entrepreneur I knew was interested in waiting 12 months to get paid. No entrepreneur I knew was interested in subjecting themselves to rigorous audits. No entrepreneur I knew was interested in undergoing new licensing certifications. For the type of money that was being offered by lenders and the audience we would have to solicit (unsophisticated first time home buyers) the "dollars didn't make sense".

Regulators turn Disorganized Opportunistic markets into **Saturated Markets** meant for the everyday consumer.

So most **Professional Entrepreneurs** I knew left.

I left.

Saturated Markets are where novices get in over their head, lose their money, complain to regulators over things they don't understand, and then as a result for their lack of abilities bring a noose around everyone's neck. The noose is for what uneducated business people (i.e. regulators) do to protect the public from unsafe practices.

This happened to me when I became a financial advisor.

I entered a financial advisory market selling investors promissory notes right after the biggest fraud in broker dealer history happened with promissory notes. This was from 2015 – 2018.

I went against my own intuition, and I paid for it. More on that later.

Saturated Markets spur over-regulation, tight money controls, caps on compensation, restrictions on creativity and high compliance costs.

If it comes after a massive fraud event all assumptions will be negative. It will not matter if the discovery comes from being honest and forth coming. I voluntarily disclosed everything I was doing in my Saturated Market.

I didn't have one compliant, one lawsuit or one nay sayer at the time over my promissory notes.

I watched the regulators bully, intimidate, and use line of questions which made people assume the worst.

When my Regulators filed their suit near the end of its statue of limitations; they inflated the number of clients. They basically doubled the number in error. An apology later didn't result in adjusting the news release. Despite the fact only 1.2mm in defaults occurred they just said it was 3.7mm.

No proof.

No evidence.

Just words.

Amazing.

When my attorney questioned them where their proof was it was amended down to 900k. Then when my attorney pushed them to account for what went to me it boiled down to 180k (the fees everyone agreed to me in writing to pay).

I watched Regulators label an audited company with leading scientist in their fields (partnered with the US Department of Agriculture for unlimited resources) a "fraud".

It is possible to make someone think something without saying it. It is also possible for someone to abuse a position of trust. Regulators are the masters at leading people where they want them to go. This is especially true if you make them angry insulting them due to their ignorance.

I recommend you be patient and nice with someone who is incompetent (Trust me I learned my lesson).

I have dealt with regulators responsible for the entire well being of our securities market *that have never even opened a business checking account*. Worse I have spoken to those deciding fines who don't even know partnerships do not file reports at the secretary of state. Imagine speaking to a regulator on international trade where the first time the person reviews an international transaction is the one you did (and it went south). The person held the job for 10 years and never saw your type of deal. Inexperience causes people like this to make negative assumptions. When confronted with lack of knowledge in their profession pride takes over. The person too proud to admit they don't understand their job tells you to "stop". The order to stop comes with a threat of "fines".

You don't want to be creative in an environment like this. The severity of ignorance is so widespread it threatens to shut you down over simple misunderstandings. If you are not a **Professional** avoid Saturated Markets.

Examples of these markets comprise our modern day US financial markets (investment advisor & broker-dealers), farming, oil and gas exploration, mining, banking & fire arms. They regulate this market down to the point where negotiating with a third party (not licensed) could cause a fine.

As government regulation removes all monetary incentives from a **Saturated Market** everyone driving innovation gradually departs. Ironically, regulation becomes the reason why the economy tanks in these areas. In true capitalism regulation does not work. True capitalism can only be balanced with stiff fines for illegal actions. Fines and civil suits for failure of businesses in the space to prevent an impossible outcome is unrealistic. Making private citizens the police does not work. Once innovators are forced to police their clients they leave. As a result, the market sags, performance suffers, and the macroeconomics begin to negatively affect the economy. Lobbyists are deployed to showcase damage. Then businesses disappear so rollbacks occur. A modern-day example of this is the proposal to unwind the US Dodd Frank Act.

Once restrictions ease it attracts innovation. The cycle begins again.

Watching the end of Disorganization is interesting. Just watch crypto currency since 2018. The money days for **Professional Entrepreneurs** in that industry is slowing coming to an end. In February 2018, JP Morgan Chase launched a coin called the JP Coin. Currently, the Securities and Exchange Commission (US) are holding open hearings. The SEC also began prosecuting cryptocurrency providers in March 2019 within the US. The time to innovate was in 2011. Bitcoin was just coming out.

My prediction is by 2024 you will need a Series 3 to trade cryptocurrency. The crypto market will become regulated by the CFTC and classified as a commodity if it does not get its own unique identifier.

The SEC is currently floating the idea of deeming crypto currency a "Utility Token".

Crypto currency's biggest issue for regulators is its difficulty to hold a single party accountable. Specifically, regulators cannot hold the creators accountable. Therefore, regulators cannot attack any one person. Regulators must attack users.

An example of this would be China making all crypto-currency transactions illegal. India has floated the same idea. In El Salvador it became legal tender in 2021. Other countries are proposing similar legislation to El Salvador.

Cryptocurrency is still a disorganized space.

In closing the most important things to take away are three (3) characteristics of opportunities: 1) Personal Reasons, 2) Disorganization and 3) Emerging Concepts.

The industry for the **Professional Entrepreneur** is irrelevant.

What matters most is the opportunity to earn money. Remember, you must know when to exit.

I can use a personal example of failure to emphasize my point.

I decided to re-enter the real estate market after shutting down my real estate company in 2011. I didn't listen to my initial gut. I was supposed to exit in 2010. I got burned by taking my remaining cash to buy more property for "steals". My inexperience with market cycles led me astray. The market would continue to plummet in 2011. It would not be until 2017 where the central Florida market would recover. The discount realtors offered me wasn't a "discount". The discount was a "market correction". In my young age, I could not recognize a pull back from a correction. I leveraged myself into 2 commercial properties and 48 parking spots. I tried to buy more real estate at the height of a market correction. As a result of burning my cash reserves to acquire more real estate I lost 14 houses. The commercial properties lost half their equity. I was in a horrible position. I had to support a 2-million-dollar mortgage for a commercial property which appraised at less than 1 million. I burnt up all my cash reserves and equity thinking property would appreciate.

I lost everything.

I was close to bankruptcy.

I failed to understand a market cycle.

I failed to properly understand the right time to exit.

This is what I want you to avoid. Learn from my failures. Learn from my oversights. Learn from actual experience.

Even negative experience is valuable. If you don't know what it's like to fail how can you ever know what it's like to succeed?

Luckily, I didn't file bankruptcy. Bankruptcy was for another time. Bankruptcy was for another lesson. That is one lesson you won't want to miss. Let's keep going.

Dreaming Past My First Success

IT WAS AN incredible feat to ride a market at 21 years old. Over 4 years I made 5.24mm in gross revenue. I wrote a list of accomplishments when I was 20. I did everything on my list by the age of 24.

The issue was…I was broke.

I met a woman who would become a major part of my life during my 2010 failures. She helped band-aid an insecurity I had. Ironically, I wouldn't recognize the reason we ended up married in 2015 until we divorced. It would be the year we married when she stopped providing that band-aid. Talk

Don't scapegoat reality for your feelings you never grow that way

about irony. It was an unfortunate time for me in 2010. Regardless she was there to witness my entire collapse. The part which inspired me to "dream past my first success" was largely due to her support.

I am still incredibly appreciative to her for that. Even after our divorce in 2019 and all the emotional turmoil I still recognize her past contributions. Some people blot out all the good with one bad. I've never been that way. It's a shame when people turn good into bad to help them self-heal.

Don't scape goat reality for your feelings you never grow that way.

Everyone searches for a reason to carry them through a hard time. Some people have God. Some people have religion. Some people have tenacity. Some people have pride.

Whatever you have make sure you hold to it. Build what I call a "conviction". What helped me hold to my conviction were old bank statements. I had banked at Wachovia before the collapse. I taped them up as a reminder I could "earn" a million dollars.

I remember taping a bank statement up that showed over 500,000 hit my bank account in one month.

I did this strategy again after I went bankrupt in 2019.

I taped my statements up and my tax returns. I reminded myself I could crack 400,000 a year. I did it consistently despite the odds.

I would let no one tell me I could not do it again. I did it before. I had to repeat it. I was "convinced".

A belief is not enough.

A belief can be changed.

A belief can be influenced.

Convictions are rooted principals you have because you "convince" yourself.

Convictions are rooted in logic, facts and proven concepts.

I had a Conviction I was simply caught up by the market. I told myself markets happen to everyone. I needed to remember who I was.

I was a **Professional Hustler.**

I saw an opportunity so I exploited it. All I needed to do to turn around my financial situation was find a similar opportunity in another market. Once I found a new market all I needed to do was the same thing I did before.

At the height of the US financial market collapse, I found another opportunity. After 4 months of searching, I discovered a void in commercial service providers offering "Commercial Real Estate Financing".

No one was doing it.

No bank, no hedge fund, no hard money lender.

The only people doing anything real estate related were private investors.

Lehman Brothers collapsed. Goldman Sachs was on the verge of bankruptcy. My close friend's crown jewel (a 50mm USD construction project in Orlando with 15mm USD in buyer's deposit) had its financing pulled by Wachovia (bought out of bankruptcy later by Wells Fargo), and Washington Mutual (a well-known mortgage lender) was closing its doors "during banking hours" out of fear everyone would pull their cash out.

It was so bad President Bush had to get on the news and tell the public to "Do not make a run on the banks."

If you do any research into our banking system you find out quickly the entire banking system is fragile. All that is needed to collapse the US monetary system is to have everyone show up simultaneously for a cash withdrawal.

> **All that is needed to collapse the US monetary system is to have everyone shows up at one time to ask for a cash withdrawal.**

Terrorist think they need to bomb the United States.

Tell the terrorist to convince the American Public their money is not available for withdrawal – then challenge them to pull it out if they are lying.

In this situation the US Monetary system would falter. That is very scary stuff. Want some simple advice?

Own precious metals and store it in your house.

The fragility of this system was challenged after the 2010 real estate collapse. This fragility made financiers virtually nonexistent.

This void created an opportunity of Disorganization. A once "Conventional Space" turned into a "Middle Space".

There was a temporary void to fill.

The central authority on financing took a vacation.

So, I decided to apply for the temp work offered to a **Professional Hustler.**

I located a small Angel Investment Group in 2010. This group had access to a tiny, licensed lender in California. The group didn't have much money. One of their main capital backers was a single guy. He had a 10mm USD Certificate of Deposit.

For me and you that's a lot.

For a person trying to do commercial financing it's not even a drop in the bucket.

Ironically in 2010, 10mm was perceived as a lot of money. The banks had no business appetite for real estate lending, so people were desperate.

People were so desperate for financing they paid "upfront fees" to anyone who could show them a tangible source.

If you could show a "proof of funds" the people wrote a check. If the only thing stopping a ***Hustler*** like me from getting paid was convincing a real person to show a verifiable account statement…I was in business.

I had negative bank accounts. My mother paid for my magic jack. My cell phone turned off.

I had negative bank accounts. My mother paid for my magic jack. My cell phone turned off.

Back in 2010 virtual offices and VOIP numbers were a novelty. Websites were still being made by IT Professionals who charged a few thousand dollars to make you one. Having a professional looking website connoted your business had money. Most IT professionals used program interfaces called Joomla or Drupal.

The programs were for people who knew how to write code.

I found "Wix" before anyone knew what it was. For 9.99 I created a website I spent $4,500 to create 3 years earlier.

I got a 1-800 number (something only available by major carriers at hugely expensive costs) for a whopping 7.99 a month (thanks Ring Central).

I rented a virtual office at $50 USD a month in a premier downtown location. I sent my mail to a private PO Box Place that was the first place in New York City to offer a physical address (with a suite number in lieu of PO Box). Doing this deal made it look like I had two offices. I had one office in Orlando that you could visit. I had another office in New York that you could call and send mail to.

My appearance was impeccable.

All for less than $100.

For 90 days I worked my tail off. The first 30 days I had no hits because no one heard of me. In the second 30 days one of my old contacts reached out to me about a Chiropractor well known in the city. He ended up committing suicide so out of respect I'll just call him the "chiropractor".

The chiropractor had over 2mm USD a year in revenues, been in business for nearly 15 years, had his own radio station channel, and cash reserves in excess of 100,000.

The bank had recently cut all his lines of credits. The bank even canceled business loans contractually obligated to due to the financial collapse.

He needed 200,000 to expand his practice.

I called up a few of my buddies from real estate that still had money and told them to take a look at it. They loved it.

My lender in California had solvency but didn't want to over extend itself in Florida. I asked if I brought the money to lend to the practice would they allow me to represent that the lender successfully funded the deal?

The lender told me yes if I paid them a processing fee. I agreed to the processing fee.

I put together a no brainer deal and gave him a 75,000 first tranche (with my buddies coming up with the cash), another 40,000 second tranche and then the rest based on him successfully illustrating growth.

I closed the deal 15 days into my 4th month (Day 105), got the reference, and they gave me the track record to tell people I could close a "real" deal.

I was suddenly the gatekeeper to the only thing available in a depressed market.

An actual financing source.

With charisma, credibility, and evidence of my performance I blew anyone out in the market that couldn't prove they did something in "today's market".

I had negative bank accounts. My mother paid for my magic jack. My cell phone turned off.

Bankers with 20 year resumes were irrelevant. The attitude was "What can you do now and what have you done since the collapse?"

Yesterday's market didn't matter. No one wanted to hear about the deals done under old rules. People wanted to know about what people could do in a market no one had ever seen.

You were good as your last deal.

That's a perfect performance based scenario.

I talked down 20-year resumes by posing simple questions. Questions like "Are you sure he's just not out of a job and trying to get money to pay his bills?" or "Did you see what they funded after the financial collapse?" or my favorite "Can he provide you an actual reference of someone who got funded within the last 30 days?"

These were powerful questions none of my competitors could answer.

Who do you think was successful at getting business?

Did I mention I made no upfront money on the chiropractor deal?

Remember, you have to be performance based. Back in the old financing days you would be lucky if you received 3%.

I received 25% of the money I attracted in 2011.

Remember what I said about multiples?

I gained a "reference" which is more valuable than the hefty performance fee.

I used that "reference" to blow away my -300 USD bank account to $79,000 in upfront fees in April 2011, about $40,000 in May, and level off another $80,000 or so in June.

I took in maybe 25 deals after my first deal. I only funded successfully two (2) of those deals. It wasn't about the amount I funded. It was the fact I "could" fund something. Everyone knew it. I had references.

> **I used that "reference" to blow away my -300 USD bank account to $79,000 in upfront fees in April 2011**

Even if it was a slim chance people were still willing to pay. At the end of the day, I got some performance in an impossible market. Say what you want, some performance was better than zero performance.

It might have been low odds, but it was better than no odds.

In this process I learned how much to charge. Don't charge too much for a low chance of success. Never take someone's last dime. That's immoral and wrong.

I didn't make a million dollars.

I didn't develop a legacy brand.

I did make over $200,000 during the worst financial market since the great depression.

> **I made over $200,000 during the worst financial market since the great depression.**

So I would say it was a pretty good year.

After I lost everything only six people stayed in my corner.

Standing by me professionally were two brothers (I have five in total), my close friend (who became an adopted brother for helping me out of a tough spot), my mother, my pops and an amazing woman.

We don't do things alone. Make sure you find a support system to encourage you. As amazing as the things I did were, it wouldn't be possible without key people in my corner.

I would have been homeless twice in my life if it wasn't for other people. Make sure you get the right people in your life. I'll talk about how to recognize those people later.

In this chapter what I am showing you is how there are opportunities in every market. These opportunities allow you to earn money.

Remember this book is not about creating a vast business empire. <u>This book is about understanding how a **Professional Hustler** earns a living</u>. The living of a **Professional Hustler** is good in any market.

Professional Hustlers can be **Professional Entrepreneurs** too.

Think about it. I was someone who was down and out. Despite my opportunity's end in one market, I could still use my resources in another market. As a **Professional Hustler** I could find an opportunity in another market.

I need you to understand something important. The name of the business I formed to support my services for less than $100 you never heard of. The name is not important. There is a reason why it's not important. **Professional Entrepreneurs** are not **Businessmen / Businesswomen**. We are not people who build business brands like Facebook, Wal-Mart, Apple, or have incredible stories about Versace's empire.

<u>Business people can be Entrepreneurs but it is not required.</u>

<u>Similar, Hustlers can be Entrepreneurs but it is not required.</u>

Business people build brands, expand markets, and create household names. **Businessmen** and **Businesswomen** come out with products that the market accepts. Sometimes their product is just your next "toilet" or a "sports drink". There are a million of those products. Sometimes the product is the Apple I-phone – pure innovation. Sometimes the market doesn't require innovation.

What made the new I-Phone dominate an established blackberry market?

A **Businessman** or **Businesswoman**, that's what.

<u>Not every Entrepreneur is a Businessman or Businesswoman.</u>

<u>Not every Businessman or Businesswoman is an Entrepreneur.</u>

Who put together people to finish the deal for a company to qualify for NASDAQ?

A **Hustler** put that deal together.

<u>Not every Entrepreneur is a Hustler.</u>

<u>No every Hustler is an Entrepreneur.</u>

Sometimes both are Professionals and sometimes both are not.

Each party is mutually exclusive but if these two combine into one person…you get a Lori Grenier (look her up she's with QVC).

Business people and entrepreneurs are usually different.

Entrepreneurs are great at exploiting opportunities in deals to make money. Most of the times incorporated entrepreneurs are niche entities (Filed LLCs or Corporations) that earn money given a certain set of market conditions.

Typically when market conditions change an incorporated entrepreneur or hustler closes.

Businessmen and **Businesswomen** <u>don't allow market change to dictate closing their business</u>. Business people evolve their company to accommodate the market (at least good ones) and these people stay in business.

That's why one of the fundamental differences in Business People and **Professional Entrepreneurs** is a very distinct characteristic. <u>The characteristic that separates</u> **Businessmen and Businesswomen** from **Professional Entrepreneurs** and **Professional Hustlers** is distinct. **Professional Entrepreneurs** open and close lots of corporate entities in their career. This is especially true with **Professional Hustlers**.

Businessmen and Businesswomen do not open and close high volumes of corporate entities. They build them to a certain point and either 1) publicly list them, 2) sell them or 3) merge them into a larger company.

Novices interpret multiple opening and closings as failed businesses or failed ventures.

Not true.

<u>The opportunity I presented you about my upfront fee model only existed when no financing existed</u>.

I created no brand, just a solution to a temporary problem.

When financing is plentiful this model would not work. It would fail. The problem does not exist anymore.

I cannot as an individual compete against Bank of America.

I cannot as an individual compete against a Hedge Fund Market that cash advances someone in 24 hours with no questions asked (literally just 3 months bank statements).

I am one person.

I am a **Professional Hustler**.

I am also a **Professional Entrepreneur.**

I can compete when mainstream people bow out. I can compete when no one with a 50 year reputation is assisting people with an everyday need.

That's easy.

That's Disorganization.

That's when the only competition is a bunch of one man / woman bands parading around.

Professional Entrepreneurs identify opportunities in disorganized markets. Once identified, the **Professional Entrepreneur** takes advantage of this disorganized market until his or her time runs out.

When your time runs out, you must know how to exit. Remember, you are there for "Opportunity" not the "Business".

Opportunity is why I became a Master Project Manager (MPM). Opportunity is why I obtained my Bachelor's in Project Management. I love the formal definition of a Project.

The formal definition of a <u>Project</u> – a temporary endeavor undertaken to accomplish a specific goal with a definitive start and end.

Professional Entrepreneurs really are "Project Managers". Each opportunity is a project. Each project will end.

Projects do not repeat.

Businesses repeat. Businesses have repetitive activities that have cycles and functions that never end.

If you are only a **Professional Hustler,** you don't open businesses you provide solutions to problems and earn money. If you are a **Professional Entrepreneur,** you open niche businesses to service a narrow opportunity. <u>If you make your project or hustle into a business, it will fail if you are not a</u> **Businessman** <u>or</u> **Businesswoman**. Find the project that serves the

> Find the project that serves the opportunity and finish it until its completion.

opportunity and finish it until its completion. As a **Professional Hustler** incorporate businesses to serve your tax purposes or shield you from legal liabilities. If you have no tax purpose or are not concerned with legal issues don't incorporate a business. I have done plenty of unincorporated structures. Unincorporated structures are "Partnerships" and "Joint Ventures".

If you are a **Professional Entrepreneur** open-up a bit coin mining location service company to companies departing China. Your market will last for the duration Chinese firms are making their exodus. Once the market normalizes your business will probably become obsolete. Close it.

Once you complete your project, the **Professional Entrepreneur** closes their project out and exits.

Know when to close your project and move on to the next one.

If you are a **Businessman** or **Businesswoman,** make sure you build a brand that outlives your project, learn the market, and adjust your brand as the market evolves. If you don't you will be one of those people who do 1mm in revenue and then make zero sales 60 days later when the market shifts.

Learn from my mistakes.

Learn from the failure to differentiate the "opportunity" from the "business".

Learn how to celebrate what you are.

Learn how to celebrate your *profession*.

Learn how to celebrate you as a **Professional Entrepreneur**.

Also, learn how to protect yourself if someone comes along who doesn't understand what you're doing.

Becoming a Professional Entrepreneur not Just an Entrepreneur

Let me pose a very straight question.

What's the difference of a "Professional" and an "Unprofessional"?

Think about it.

What makes you a **Professional**?

What is the difference between a **Professional Hustler** and a **Professional Entrepreneur**?

When I first started out, I made a comment. I called myself a *Hustler*. To a large extent that was true. You see *Hustlers* have charisma, wit, great speaking abilities, and usually a few credible verifiable facts.

Professionals have something called "credentials".

So a **Professional** is your doctor, your lawyer, your accountant, your tax adviser, your stock broker or your insurance agent. These individuals are usually fee based individuals who have established the right to charge you a fee due to a very complex system.

A complex system is the US legal system. Did you know to sue someone most of the time it only cost a few hundred dollars? Does that sound shocking to you? It should. The filing fees are always small. The payment for someone else's time is not small. When you see a large legal bill (like 20,000 USD) usually 100% of the bill is for someone's time.

Nothing else.

A lot of attorneys will bill you $350 USD per hour. I have one attorney who bills $650 an hour. Sometimes all they do is talk to you. Nothing tangible really happens during these conversations except good advice. They will give you good advice. I'm not saying a good conversation with an attorney is not productive. When your freedom is at stake, you should pay what you have in order to get good representation. I had to pay $100,000 to an attorney when I was indicted of bank wire fraud earlier this year. An attorney is important in this instance. When someone is suing you for $500,000 USD what's $40,000 in legal fees if you get the claim dismissed? If a District Attorney alleges something which carries jail time it's important to get it cleared up by a good attorney. A person sued me for $1,300,000 once. I paid roughly $44,000 in legal fees. At the end of 8 hours of mediation, I paid a single $80,000 settlement fee and the case dismissed. I got a general release of any wrongdoing. I even got a signed declaration that everything he said was "bogus".

It still cost me a grip to deal with.

Legal fees pile up when an attorney files a motion or does a deposition. Court hearings in practice are not long. I've had a few hearings in my time. The judge listens but just wants the brass tacks of everything. They do not allow attorneys to give dramatic Perry Mason style speeches most of the time. Most rarely do. Filing a motion is work. I have seen expert attorneys spend about 6 hours filing a motion, 5 hours doing research, and maybe call around for another 4 hours trying to make sure they prepare properly. During this time the attorneys are giving you their undivided attention. In one day they charge you 15 hours multiplied by $350. In this situation your bill is roughly $5,250.00. Imagine your legal bill if this attorney repeats this situation five more times?

Every court system in the United States allows you to file Pro Se (basically file or defend yourself without representation). The only exception to this is with incorporated entities like corporations. Corporations must hire attorneys. People are different. My personal experience is Judges are usually hostile in this situation. I once tried to evict someone Pro Se. Literally the judge told the tenant they had no legal right to be there but the only reason why he was dismissing the case was because I filed wrong. He straight up told the defendant if I sued her properly she would lose. She sat there blinking like a deer standing in head lights. The judge chastised her because he sympathized with me. Then the Judge told me to go get an attorney. After he kicked both of us out, I lost the case. Therefore, I do not recommend filing Pro Se. The US legal system is based on doing it right not being right.

> **The US legal system is based on doing it right not being right.**

No one files Pro Se because civil and criminal procedure is so technical. If you do one thing wrong in the legal system (procedurally) the whole case is akin to pissing into the wind.

You can be right morally but wrong legally. Is that fair? Is that moral? Is that right? Maybe not.

But that's the way it is.

The way our legal system is gives you one giant hurdle in your career as a **Professional Entrepreneur**. The giant hurdle you have in your career as a **Professional Entrepreneur** is coming up with enough money to survive litigation.

Remember the litigation hurdle.

The same concept applies to accountants and tax professionals. These people bill by the hour to run up bills based on hourly rates. It can get out of hand quickly. The second biggest hurdle you must learn as a **Professional Entrepreneur** is a simple.

Make sure you educate yourself to properly have correct financials. Promptly file taxes. Sound simple? It is simple. Lots of people experience misrepresentation claims because they fail to do correct financials.

Improper financials drags you to your worst and best friend (all at once). The **Legal Professional**. Don't go the Pro Se route. Do not ignore the importance of an attorney. You will end up like me. Remember my example of filing an eviction in a county court. The correct thing is a civil ejection in federal court. Learning cost you time and money you don't have.

> **Lots of people experience *misrepresentation* claims because they fail to do correct financials.**

I'm pretty sure you want to know what type of credentials you need as a **Professional Entrepreneur**. Do you need to be an attorney? An accountant? A doctor?

Not quite.

Don't get me wrong. If you are any of those your life and career as a **Professional Entrepreneur** will be significantly easier. I would argue an attorney, who has it in them to be an entrepreneur, has the best chance of smashing it.

I say this because of a very simple reason.

When a Legal Professional is an Entrepreneur they eliminate the largest contingent cost. The cost eliminated is unnecessary "legal bills". An attorney is the only person who can legally beat up on someone. Attorneys are the only people who can crush people financially (literally). I always say if I could do it all over again I would have become a Professional Attorney instead of a Professional Financial Advisor.

Important Points on your Giant Hurdle (Litigation)

I spent over $200,000 USD in legal bills (someone's time) in a 24-month period. Various issues always came up handling money. The results on all these cases were what I knew from the beginning.

My current case is similar.

The people didn't have a claim and these litigants were pulling me into something unfairly. The entire basis of my current situation is things I already settled.

I settled one case concerning elderly abuse on a man I never met, never accepted a dime from, on a transaction not paid for, when he wasn't my client. I never directly emailed nor spoke to this person (personally or through the phone). I settled it for less than 15% of his claimed damages. Do you think someone who honestly believes I am guilty of something would settle for that low? I mean use common sense.

On another claim, I provided bank statements, transaction records showing the return of money, wire receipts, and even my attorneys communication with her legal team she was paid back all her $600,000 from various issuers.

She still complained to the regulators and lied about it.

When I gave the evidence to the regulators to substantiate my defense, they referred it to a district attorney because the woman kept hounding people.

She was upset about the amount of her return.

The official stance…criminal doesn't talk with civil sorry we don't have access to that information. We plead it anyway sorry.

Amazing.

Let's pretend you are the person who is saying I owe you money. You say I lost you $10 because you found my name somewhere on a document you considered to be "material" in your decision process. Mind you that you used an attorney to advise you (and sued your attorney until you found out he was broke). Now you turn your attention towards me. You drag everything out for 2 years and at the end of a 2 year saga you tell me to give you a $1.50. With that $1.50 you prepared to walk away with no strings attached. Does this make any sense to you? Especially when you either 1) had to give away $0.50 (a 33% success fee) or 2) spent about $1.00 in legal fees (so you net out maybe 5% of what you thought).

It doesn't make sense does it?

That's litigation for you.

The other example I had during this period was paying just to get a case dismissed with Prejudice based on zero merits. The last bill I received for the one with "zero merit" was a whopping $20,000 USD. It cost me nearly $50,000 to defend nothing. Literally the guy had nothing.

For my indictment I faced charges of bank wire fraud because after five years of detective work no one could find evidence of securities fraud, embezzlement or theft. Therefore, all that good work wasn't going to go to waste.

Here we see he paid a third-party professional to report his assets under management but they should have been classified as assets under advisement. Paying a professional to do something he didn't know how to do isn't an excuse.

Let's get him for a technicality on improper asset reporting.

This is the type of stuff that can happen when you are a complete ass hole to people looking for what happened to money that went overseas without use of legal professional to supervise a transaction.

Why go for the truth when you can just get something put to bed on a technicality?

My penalty?

One hundred thousand dollars, false press, attempts to ruin my reputation, sticking on technicalities to teach you a lesson and getting locked up with some pretty dark folks to teach me some respect for authority.

Crazy right?

Legal bills will sink any endeavor you do as a **Professional Entrepreneur**. Be particular how you handle your deals. My good attorney friend use to always say "Let's face it – NOBODY LIKES GETTING SUED. And you can bet that if you are in business someone will sue you. It is not a question of "if," but "when."

This is a view held by many other attorneys.

The reason people get sued is easy. It is very easy file a civil lawsuit in America. Anyone can "allege" something. Proving your allegation in a court of law differs from alleging your allegation. There is something called a "frivolous lawsuit"; however, you still have to prove its "frivolous". You must answer any compliant that comes your way. If you don't answer the compliant guess what you get?

A Default Judgment.

What is a Default Judgment?

A Default Judgment is when another party (usually the defendant) fails to respond to a legally served (usually by process server) complaint. In a compliant the defendant has a certain amount of time (by law) to respond to the allegations. If the defendant properly receives notice of the compliant and ignores it – the plaintiff is eligible to put in a "Motion for Default".

You can overturn default judgment through appeal; however, it is very difficult and costly. Courts dislike defendants who just ignore petitions. Appellate courts in practice don't like to overturn other judges' rulings. Overturning a judges' ruling implies incompetence or bad conduct. Judges are very careful about soiling each others' reputations. There has to be "clear" evidence that they did something in error by the ruling judge. The only Motions to Set Aside a Judgment (after the fact) I have seen go over well are ones where the judge just made a routine ruling based on improper jurisdiction (where Defendant can show that Plaintiff cited a contract in their compliant for business subject to another jurisdiction but withheld or failed to point out improper venue) or a complete failure by a process server to do their job correctly (basically not the judge's fault since he would have never made the ruling based on a false statement of another person).

If you think you can be clever and just file a "Motion to Dismiss" to dismiss something I have news for you. One important factor I learned about the famous "Motion to Dismiss" strategy is its assumption of truth.

In a Motion to Dismiss the judge is required to assume everything filed is true. Based on the truth it is your job to showcase that while all the facts in the compliant are true; the truth creates a violation in basic civil procedure. As a result, based on the truth the case is dismissed and must be filed again properly.

You do not win in a Motion to Dismiss. You delay in a Motion to Dismiss in my experience.

Sound tricky?

It is.

This is not legal advice. I am telling you my experience with different situations over the years. Laws change and so does civil procedure. I am not qualified to tell you one way or another; what is "Current Law" versus "Outdated Law". I am merely illustrating why you need to have good counsel advise you properly in a bad situation.

Categories of a Professional Entrepreneur

You attain **Professional Entrepreneur** by being one of the following persons:

1) Carrying an actual Professional License.
2) Carrying a recognized third party certification in an applicable field (I.E. qualifying for Errors and Omissions Insurance).
3) Showcasing verifiable businesses that was / is profitable on at least two (2) occasions (to eliminate the one time wonders).
4) Successfully filing a patent through the USPTO (think inventors).
5) Obtaining industry awards for recognized talent (think singers, artists, entertainers or comedians)

That's it.

I obtained number 1 (Carrying a Professional License) thorough my Series 65 and my Life & Health State Insurance License. I obtained number 2 (Obtaining Professional Certifications) through my Master Project Manager (MPM), Master Financial Planner (MFP) and Accredited Financial

Analyst (AFA). I formed businesses that on their tax returns could show number 3 (I can produce at least five tax returns where I record taxable profit). I also worked with three (3) separate businesses that obtained three (3) separate patent portfolios on "relevant" items to fulfill Number 4 (Filing a patent through the USPTO). One patent was in the graphics industry (it won the SGIA product of the year award in 2008, solved carpel tunnel syndrome in applications and reduced labor hours by 50%), the second patent portfolio was in biotechnology (sequencing anti fungal properties in cash crops that are important to the US economy – one has a NY Times article written about it) and the final patent was in payment settlements on foreign currencies (where the law firm Greenberg Traurig wrote an opinion letter they felt the company's patent was one of the most important patents ever issued on foreign currency conversions). These were the companies the SEC said weren't real companies (I know right that's some real good detective work SEC). I've done everything to meet the definition of a **Professional Entrepreneur** except number 5 (obtain industry awards).

> **Anything that is not in the five categories above really puts you in the category of a *Hustler***

Anything that is not in the five categories above puts you in the category of a *Hustler*.

Hustlers are not bad.

Remember, we need *Hustlers*.

Hustlers are the fires that spark with no tinder. *Hustlers* have components to them that can greatly propel a business. Sometimes even a **Professional Entrepreneur** doesn't have the skill set to launch a business successfully.

Hustlers are usually the only thing that makes a start up go.

Professional Entrepreneurs that want to do start ups must be a *Hustler* or partner with a *Hustler*. Otherwise your start up will never take off no matter how opportunistic the opportunity is.

How do you get someone to give you $100,000 on a pure idea with no track record? How do you get someone to give you $100,000 with no security?

How do you get someone to give you $100,000 with no tangible asset?

How do you get someone to give you $100,000 with no way of getting paid back if what you say does not work?

How do you get someone to give you $100,000 based on their belief in you alone?

Do you want to know the straight forward answer to these questions?

It's called you *hustle* it in.

That's what I was good at. You will see my track record in detail shortly. My record is 9-5-1. I have lost roughly 3.1mm and made roughly about 13.3mm in gross revenue. It is not illegal to lose money. Despite what people feel it is not illegal. This is a risk we must all take if we want to make more than $300 bucks on $10,000. Do

I'm slightly better than a coin toss in the most aggressive asset class imaginable.

everyone a favor and don't accuse people if money gets lost. If you know they didn't steal it and can prove it save everyone heart ache. Personally, I'm a little better than a coin toss in the most aggressive asset class imaginable. I am the definition of high risk high returns. Some call me a gambler. I am by definition a Venture Capitalist if classified as anything when choosing investments.

According to a Quartz article, where Bill Gates stated VC Firm performance was dismal at best (www.qz.com), the Kauffman Foundation was cited for its investment in VC Firms over a 20-year period. In 2012, Kauffman looked at the returns and found in the long run VC firms returned on average only 1.31 times what they invested (throughout this 20-year period). When a few exceptional performers were stripped out of Kauffman's portfolio, the return rate was even worse. That was despite billions of dollars being invested. As many as three quarters of venture backed startups failed outright.

Leading experts, that accepted billions of dollars from 1992 to 2012 for my type of asset class, sported a whopping 25% success rate.

According to Kauffman what does what I do mean?

Leading experts, that accepted billions of dollars from 1992 to 2012 for my type of asset class, sported a whopping 25% success rate.

You may look at my performance and say "Chris 9-5-1 means you are 60.0% accurate not counting your tie. That is not that great. You are basically a safer coin toss."

If you say that I say in response, "Gent / Lady, based on my track record I select successful ventures correctly more than twice the rate of leading VC Firms. I had access to less than 1% of their liquidity and none of their help. I have returned a gross earnings rate nearly 5x the rate of what was allocated by my competition."

My job is not to make sure the revenue numbers end up being reported as profitable. My job is not to assist what the business does with the revenue I generate. I have never been the chief cook and bottle washer in practice. I have always been a **Professional Hustler** whose role was the "opportunity" not the "business".

The role of the "business" I left to other people. The only company I owned entirely outright (with my brother) was the Mortgage and Real Estate Company (5.24mm over 30 months. By all definitions that was an excellent win). I personally had a time share company that went bust (I personally lost $135,000).

A separate lifestyle membership company I purchased a small stake in and agreed to temporarily be the CFO in went under during COVID. That company lost 350,000 of investor money despite doing nearly three quarters of a million in sales. The market ran that one to the ground. It was located in Florida when the pandemic shut the market down. Needless to say that person filed a FINRA dispute claim 3 years after I closed my practice. This happened despite him never being a client. He never spoke to me. He has no contract with my signature on it for managing his money. His money was 100% accounted for. It was used to pay employee wages for nearly 20 people. I think he sent me two emails. I simply thanked him. I was 1 of 5 officers in the company. I"m still trying to figure why I am named in that one. That's a civil suit for you.

In each year I have always earned a good living. That's the point of this book. The year preceding my bankruptcy I grossed a lot. I made over $150,000.00 to my individual account and over $500,000 to my personal, corporate account (remember tax purposes). **In all the wins and all the losses I still did my part to earn good money**. I finished my bankruptcy year at $113,000 gross with after taxable deductions reducing my taxable burden to around $85,000. Remember, companies do not comprise one person. There are multiple roles, positions, jobs and processes. No one person is responsible for everything in business. I earned my six-figure compensation in every deal they involved me. I never broke any laws. I never cheated anyone. I never did the opposite of what they signed on a piece of paper.

When charges couldn't be drawn up for theft, embezzlement, securities fraud or basically any real charge you would want to hang someone for in my pleading they found a technical way to charge me.

No one is perfect and neither am I.

This is my opinion and many other legal attorney opinions I have spoken too.

When people from my past asked, "What do you think about Chris?"

In general I like to think the ones that lost money will at most say, "It didn't work out the way he said it would. I don't think he's not a bad guy but I'm not happy with him."

The biggest cheap shot I would expect is, "I believed and trusted in him. Because I trusted him I lost. I shouldn't have believed in him so much."

I've never been sued by a former partner, former company I worked with, former shareholder or former joint venture party (as of my writing this book). I've had a big entity try and strong-arm ownership of a fund by claiming something technical on one of my companies (but leaving my personal name off the suit). I've been sued quite a few times in the past. They usually were from people who I had no relationship with. I've won every case except two. I don't count the ones where I signed a confession of judgment on a cash advance. I borrowed money and couldn't pay it back. Cash advances were simple transactions that didn't require litigation. The cases I lost were usually because of money issues or not even knowing the case existed (the dreaded Default Judgment).

My ex-wife got me on that technicality.

Usually, I was sued by people recommended by third parties who I never met.

Rarely has anyone who looked me in my face, shook my hand, and spent time with me later spit in my face and said, "I'm suing you".

If you are only a Hustler, chances are you do not have intrinsic credibility.

69

I don't think people would say anything else beside what I've said above. You never know though. I don't know people's hearts. I only know my heart. You have to look at yourself in the mirror. If you can't stand the image you are looking at, then you can't be in this profession.

I sleep well at night. I know what I did and I can live with it. I never conspired or planned anything. Neither will you when you get sued. So don't beat yourself up.

I have a news flash for you.

People will make things up about you if they lose money. This is true if the person who takes their does not give it back to them.

This type of lawsuit is quite common.

The narration goes, "You introduced me to the opportunity, so you make it right. I don't care if you didn't take the money."

Make sure you get indemnification waivers for this situation. People sign them and they provide defenses for you.

If you are a person that does multi level marketing, relies upon fortune five hundred companies' credibility, or receives a 1099 for doing side hustle – you may not be a **Professional Entrepreneur.**

Depending on how you do things with those situations you *might be an entrepreneur* – but it depends on what you do. If you are an affiliate marketer through some platform this *probably means you're just hustling*. Nothing wrong with that. I respect you to your core.

You're not an *entrepreneur* for hustling.

Hustlers are resourceful people. **Hustlers** earn money based on other people's credibility. **Hustlers** *are resourceful enough to put a deal together.* If you are only a Hustler, chances are you do not have intrinsic credibility. That's okay. I hustled when I was 20 without a track record. I had to hustle when I was 20. I had nothing of substance to show people. That is why Hustler C (remember the CPA from my real estate days) was so important. **He was a 40-year-old former CPA who had some verifiable facts about him.** Even then, Hustler C was still a hustler. Hustler C was not an Entrepreneur. How do I know? Hustler C never opened up a successful business after our pre 2010 real estate market. Last time I checked he was a "Life Coach" on LinkedIn. Do you know what is a "Life Coach" is? Look it up.

I think you can figure out what those people are.

Remember do not to fail to identify yourself. That is how you will lose money. Identify failures waste time. Not every company I did worked out. I was not and have never been a **Businessman.**

My bankruptcy was a direct result of trying to be a **Businessman** in two industries I had no experience in. If you didn't read the *Richest Man In Babylon* you should read it. Study the Five Laws of Gold. I ignored a key law.

> **Not every company I did worked out. I was not and have never been a Businessman**

"Gold slippeth away from the man who invests it in businesses or purposes with which he is not familiar or which not approved by those skilled in its keep."

I knew nothing about timeshare but decided I wanted to get into it. In my ignorance I thought I could just get someone "smarter" than me. I wanted to make 10mm USD not 1mm. I also decided I wanted to be the executive of an international biotechnology conglomerate. So I closed my financial advisor at a time when I had grown my revenue each year it was open ($238,106 to $342,317.06 to $462,300.57 to my final year of $568,819.61). I abandoned an entrepreneurial based endeavor that generated me over 1.6mm to try out something I knew nothing about. The result was bankruptcy.

I violated an age-old rule.

I encourage you to avoid violating the rule of betting everything on something you know nothing about.

Embrace what you are and optimize what you are good at.

Hustlers can make good money. *Hustlers* can earn six figures every year. *Hustlers* who lack experience generally have no real substance aside from charisma, presence and one or two verifiable facts. Do not turn a hustle into a business.

> **A real performer tells you the odds. You play by them.**

I was a *Hustler.*

I still am.

Any person who tells you everything they touch turns to gold is a liar. A real performer tells you the odds. You play by them. All you can do is "Win more than you lose".

All that matters is your record.

What's my record with doing deals profitable?

I'll list them:

Revenue Wins

Real Estate & Mortgage Company – Did 5.24mm over 30 months

Financing Company - $350,000 in one year

Forex & Trading Company (Non Owner) - $200,000 USD per year for 2 years ($400,000 total)

Financial Advisor (Founder) – 1.6mm USD over 40 months

Mortgage Correspondent Lender – Paid out in excess of $200,000 over 18 months after raising $500,000 in working capital and in excess of 2mm USD for solvency

Project Management Firm (Current) – Earn over $600,000 in gross revenue over 24 month period during COVID Pandemic outbreak.

Revenue Losses

Graphics Company – Lost Money 3 years in a row. Total money lost little north of $400,000. (Might be profitable in future as it's still open)

Mining & Exploration Company – Lost 1.2mm on failed exploration in Africa. Victim of theft and fraud. Ended up indicted for allegations which could not be proven in civil court. Elevated to criminal. Though not formally charged for theft, embezzlement, or securities fraud technicalities enabled bank fraud charges.

Timeshare Sales Company – The Company did about 730,000 in sales over 12 months. I over leveraged the firm based on projections and did not understand I was at the tail end of a dying market. When the market collapsed amid an RCI 800mm loss it left me holding the bag. COVID 19 sealed its fate (try running a time share company in Florida when 94% of all travel stops). The loss resulted in a lack of third-party fulfillment on vacation packages and a complete abandonment of back end support. Personal loss was approximately $135,000 on this one and the single investor loss all 350k. Default of business debt from banks & financing companies more than $100,000.

Revenue Ties

<u>Wholesale Tire Company</u> – Cash on cash return was $180,000 in and $216,000 out. There was an outstanding profit of about $112,000 of investor money in a tire transaction. The transaction later turned into a fraudulent transaction. I earned about $45,000 on the deal. Technically, no monies were lost but they lost profit and investor had to cover fees for my time. Total fraud conducted was over 20mm USD. I recovered majority of funds due to smart structuring and my lessons from the past. I was actually the only person to recover any funds. Two people went against my advice on how to structure the deal properly. <u>One lost 2.4mm and the other lost $300,000. Know how to get yourself out of a bad situation.</u> I count this one as a tie.

Revenue Record 5-3-1

Market Wins

<u>Biotechnology Firm</u> – Secured USDA Partnership until commercialization. Estimated Market Cap at IPO 150mm. This market cap was supported by raising 1.1mm in working capital, 2.5mm in solvency capital and obtaining a Best Efforts underwriting commitment from an offshore US Bank for 100mm USD.

<u>Foreign Currency Conversion Patent Company</u> – Signed partnership with a private company who holds a contract with a publicly traded company to payout 1.7mm USD within 18 months   3.5% royalty thereafter.

<u>Hemp Agricutlure Biotech Company</u> – Invested into a pre-ipo stock company at $0.05 per share. Made subsequent investments at $0.25, $0.30 and $0.40. Realized 5.2mm market gain up front with 2mm remaining shares to be sold on major stock exchange.

Market Losses

> Real Estate Trust Holdings – Lost nearly 4mm in properties in 2010

> Private Holding Company – Lost about 300,000 in ventures that have not paid out.

Market Record – 3 – 2
Total Record – 9 – 5 – 1

You will notice something very important. I win more than I lose. The wins (in terms of money) also outweigh the loss numbers. Actually, the profit amounts outweigh the loss amounts by a lot (monetarily). I have roughly a 4:1 win loss earnings ratio. I roughly earned 4 times more than I lost over my career.

You see, I have made some great success stories. I have also had failures. Because of some of my failures I have lost money. No one wants to talk about their failures. You have too. Sometimes in my failures I have lost other people's money. I wish I could say that everything works out.

The truth is not everything works out.

Two of my losses came from startups (private holding company & mining company). Start-ups by definition have about a 75% chance of failure. The market hit one of my losses (real estate holding company during housing collapse). There was nothing I could do about that one. I had lack of experience and was a victim of the market. That happens sometimes. Seasoned people lost their shirts on that one. That's probably the only one I give myself a pass on. One loss I took due to losing my identity on which type of person I was (the timeshare company). I tried going from a **Professional Entrepreneur** to a **Businessman**. Had I made better decisions the company might still be around. We experienced some heavy losses early on. I didn't know the timeshare industry's marketing tactics.

I relied upon people bigger than me and a partner who hustled me into believing he was something he was not. I was then swindled on bad marketing after making large capital investments in 3rd party resorts based on others' guarantees. Never take anyone's word for anything in Orlando Florida. Especially owners of aging resorts. Beware of Kissimmee it can be a snake pit. Certain people over there will lie through their teeth to make a buck. Timeshare is cut throat. Bad move by me. My gut was wrong on that one. I own that. COVID prevented any resuscitation. Florida was down 94% travel (as of June 2020) and COVID is not over. Great businesses are going bankrupt. A 3 year emerging company isn't going to survive this one unfortunately.

My two other losses came on international transactions. My advice about international deals is as follows, "Do not put money in a country you are not sufficiently capitalized in to aggressively have local legal attorneys apply pressure."

Foreign partners will stick you because legally they think you can't do anything. Be cautious overseas.

People in other countries do not care about the United States. If your partners are in another country and your partners don't have US Citizenship, they will completely ignore all your US legal recourse. Foreign partners will stick you because legally they think you can't do anything. Be cautious overseas. Civil law jurisdictions in practice do not recognize foreign judgments. It is meaningless what you do stateside to enforce contracts on a foreign party.

I have a saying I still think is valid today. Without something called the "Wow Effect", a start-up can expect to raise anywhere from 300,000 – 1mm USD over a 12-month cycle.

Anything else is unrealistic and not achievable. The only exceptions I personally know are those partnered with big brands (think celebrity, industry leader, famous person, former executive person at Goldman Sach's).

I changed from a *Hustler* when I obtained "credentials". I learned the value of being a **Professional.** When you do not have vast wealth to showcase your apparent success having credentials are essential. I obtained a bachelor's degree first. Then I obtained a Master Project Manager (MPM), Master Financial Planner (MFP) and an Accredited Financial Analyst (AFA) designation. Choosing to pass my Series 65 was also important in establishing my credentials. I also obtained a Life & Health license.

A license or certification is important if you lack wealth.

Take heed.

I consider myself a **Professional** because I have tangible analytical skills. I'm a **Professional** because I can do technical work. Remember *Hustlers* are people who get into stuff and capitalize.

I know how to analyze markets. I can assess deficiencies in markets gaps. I am great at spotting out lack of organization. I can meet with heads of businesses and convince people to give me an opportunity.

I differ from a *Hustler* now because I have formal education and do technically savvy things. I do not get myself into situations and capitalize.

Hustlers get themselves into situations and capitalize.

That's it.

Capitalizing is not a bad thing. Often there is a need. Find a situation to capitalize off if you want to pay your bills. Do not devalue the *Hustler*. *Most of the time people starve during a famine without a Hustler*.

> *Hustlers* get themselves into situations and capitalize. That's it.

To label yourself a **Professional Entrepreneur, or Professional Hustler** you must obtain professional designations. The credentials you attain differentiates you from other people who are just blessed with the gift of gab.

Talking and communicating is half the battle. If you cannot articulate complex ideas in simple third-grade language, you will create your own road-blocks. Take the time to avoid acronyms, avoid utilizing industry lingo, and talk in "common sense". Whenever I speak with someone I use "third-grade words".

I don't pretend to be smarter than the person. I don't say anything that is not relevant to the conversation. If you have a great accomplishment, hold it for the moment it makes sense to bring it up.

If you have built 10 houses from the ground up wait for the person to tell you they don't understand how to zone a house. Bring up the point casually. Inform them zoning is a process undertaken to ensure people follow city planning guidelines. Tell them if a person needs to rezone make sure the person sets their meeting with the local board. Walk the person through approaches at city hall. Recommend the person speak with

> To carry the label Professional Entrepreneur, it is important to obtain professional designations

the zoning department. If a person asks how you acquired knowledge tell them,

"I built 10 houses in my time and I went through it over and over. If you need help with it let me know."

If you play this interaction out, you may watch this person's eyes light up. In this instance this person will not find you boastful. This person will find you resourceful.

In this same situation if you lead a conversation with how many houses you built it may not go well. The person may think you brag a lot. You may cause intimidation. The person may not talk to you about their deal.

Do you know what is worse?

Finding out they didn't want to talk to you about houses.

Imagine wasting 30 minutes showcasing an irrelevant history to their needs.

Remember "Cost Benefit Analysis". How much does it cost you to spend your time talking about something no one cared about?

Maybe a lot.

Maybe a small deal.

Maybe a deal that was worth 1mm.

You will never know.

You won't know because you blew your opportunity. You talked about something for no reason or came off as a grand stander. Don't arbitrarily talk about things. Don't talk about things which serve no other purpose but propping you up. No one needs to hear your accomplishments for no apparent reason. Trust me, people don't care.

Professionals are great at their profession and know how to correctly assess their market.

Entrepreneurs identify situations that potentially yield opportunity in niche markets.

Hustlers find a way to insert themselves into a situation and capitalize on the fact that they are there. They use great presence and charisma to attract the attention they need. Hustlers command the room.

Both Entrepreneurs and Hustlers recognize the importance of: 1) personal reasons, 2) disorganization or 3) emerging concepts.

To launch a new concept, find a *Hustler.* If you cannot find a *Hustler* become one. If you are a *Hustler* great. If you are *Hustler* who aspires to be something more take time to get credentials. Don't divert attention away from you if pressed to showcase something tangible. Don't waste your time finding exemptions for why you do not need something (i.e. a license or certification). Just get the credential you need. You can still do all the things you usually do (i.e. have the spot-light focused on someone else) but if someone asks a straightforward question like "What makes you qualified to be here?"

You can shoot back.

"I'm the attorney."

"I'm the General Contractor."

"I'm the Accountant".

Or

"I founded the company acquired by XXX."

Do you see the value in those statements?

> **"Whenever someone says many words to answer a yes or no question they are usually full of shit."**

The value in those statements is tremendous. A person holding a credential can always justify their presence. Simple is good. Less is more. Justification with one sentence means your words have weight. You do not need a lot of words to prove your value. I have a rule. My rule is simple.

"Whenever someone says many words to answer a yes or no question they are usually full of shit."

Sorry if my words came across a little brash. These words are the truth. That last curse word is probably the only curse word you will find in this entire book. I'm using that word to emphasize the point. Don't spend 30 minutes explaining. Don't talk without taking a breath. If you are talking that long, then you probably have no value.

Always feel comfortable justifying value at a table. If you cannot say value in a few sentences, then you probably don't deserve to have a seat at the table.

Be a **Professional.**

Be an **Entrepreneur.**

Be a **Businessman** or **Businesswoman.**

Or just be a *Hustler.*

Either way, you need to know who you are. Know your place and get it done. Let's go to work **Professional Hustler.**

Getting a Taste of a Real High Yield Return

WHEN I FIRST started out exploring the concept of making money I focused on earning enough money to get by. The thought of making less fifty thousand a year was not something I could stomach. I wanted to at least earn enough money to afford the lifestyle

Your parents are the people that serve as your first role models.

my parents provided me as a youth. It's natural to think of ways to earn similar to your parents. Your parents are the people that serve as your first role models. Your parents show you their achievements. Hopefully, your parents inspire you to achieve something similar. What parents ask you to do is not viewed as impossible if their achievements are experienced first-hand. Parents are supposed to teach their children. Parents inspire children to have self-worth. Parents inspire children to achieve goals.

The way we go about achieving those standards will vary according to individualism. Parents should teach you doing something like them is not impossible. You don't have to be your "father". You don't have to be your "mother". You can be your own person.

American dreams are individual dreams.

Our country promotes being an individual. My generation (anyone born after 1980 but before 1989) lost the mantra of having society collectively tell us what we should be.

My generation was the sequel to the 1970's hippies (be free and do you).

When I first left high school, my dilemma was, "How do I make a $1,081 mortgage?" I thought about it. I didn't have an answer. I answered a question with a question. Questions always lead you to answers.

I asked myself, "How do I earn that much money?"

It is an incredibly simple question. Asking yourself the right question will get your mind working. Once your mind is working it will seek out answers. Your mind will look around at its environment. My mind looked around. What my mind saw were options I was not satisfied with. I realized we do not get paid according to our time. We get paid according to the value we provide others.

This was a new concept for me.

You need willpower to get through constant failures you experience on your search for answers. People are not born with willpower. You must train for willpower. How everyone gets it is different.

I obtained my willpower in youth.

I was part of a state championship football team (Rockledge Raiders 2001 & 2002 were Back to Back Florida State 3A Champions) which taught me good values.

As a champion my coaches ingrained work effort (diligence) and time commitment. I struggled through some hard times. God forged me through these hard times by cultivating willpower. I had intense drive because of my football experiences. I was also extreme. I would literally have rather died on the football field than miss a tackle. I was born with asthma. So that is something that could have happened. I forced myself through hard times.

I developed a very high willpower.

I always say exercise is good for people looking to be successful.

Pushing yourself through discomfort will refine and develop your willpower.

I played with the wind capacity of an average person (despite running like an Olympic athlete). Later in life I injured my lower lumbar. I tried to squat 450 lbs 10x without a belt (don't ask me why I did that I just did it). I did it 8x. On the 9th repetition my lower back wiggled like a rubber band. I was determined not to fail. I did

> **I was extreme. I would literally have rather died on the football field than miss a tackle.**

not drop the weight. I pushed the rep up with pure willpower. I racked the weight. I walked around. I looked at my older brother who was with me. I told him "I think I hurt my back".

I sat down.

I then lay back on the weight bench.

Do you know what happened when I lay down? All the inflammation happened. I was so inflamed in my lower back when I tried to sit up spider webs of light filled my vision. I passed out. My brother had to call an ambulance. That is the only time I ever got hurt lifting weights. I was 32 years old. When I went to the emergency room it amazed people at the description of what happened. An ER person told me something similar happened the week before I arrived. The difference was the person who came in before me didn't finish his repetition. His situation paralyzed him from the waist down. A person who lacked the willpower to push his final repetition up now sits in a wheelchair.

Willpower prevents you from breaking.

By God's grace my raw willpower resulted in me not becoming paralyzed. It took me 12 hours to sit up again. I spent the next 2 weeks with a cane. I was nursed back to health. It was a full 2 months before I walked normally again. It was 3 months before I could do any form of lifting.

The injury led me to a discovery. Willpower led me to a true example of my body adapting to stress. My body adapted to stress while I played football. My body adapted through extreme conditioning. The adaptation my body accomplished was very interesting.

When I injured my lower back, the emergency technician introduced a contrast to my body. The purpose of contrast was to make it easier on the imaging to see injuries (ruptures, internal bleeding, et cetera). The reason hospital staff were so hesitant to discharge me was they had a very odd reading. There was a mass of

I literally demanded my body to physically evolve through extreme trauma.

contrast on my lower left kidney. The mass went all the way up to my heart. No doctor had ever seen anything like it. It took them 8 hours to figure out what it was. Do you know what it was? My body literally created new veins. The purpose of the veins are apparently to increase the blood flow to my heart. As far as I know I am the only person in the world to have blood flowing directly from my kidney to my heart.

Willpower conditions you to withstand things others cannot.

You need willpower to withstand things that come at you as a **Professional Hustler** and **Professional Entrepreneur.**

I stressed my cardiovascular system so much, despite my asthma (I still have it) my body engineered another way to get proper oxygen to circulate through my body. My body does this by pumping blood faster to my heart. By having a lifeline go straight from its toxicity center to the heart I can increase my clean blood flow. My body differs completely from a normal person in this respect.

I literally demanded my body to physically evolve through extreme trauma. Trauma is important to accommodate full blown sprinting, distance running, and other high stress activities.

People cannot withstand trauma without willpower. It is traumatic dealing with a failed business. It is very traumatic being sued by people who called you friend. It is extremely traumatic to be accused of something you can prove is not true.

At the heart of all these traumatic events is money loss. You will lose money choosing this career.

This career is not for the faint at heart. This career is not for those who do not train their willpower.

I have not used my asthma pump since I was 18 years old. I discarded my pump at 18. I could not join the Air Force if I had to use an inhaler. After football I had drive to pass the air force physical without my pump. I strengthen my lungs and kept my work ethic up. I don't know when my body made this change. I imagine it was somewhere between 18 and 32.

> **I do difficult things because willpower is something exercised. Willpower is weak without constant stress tests.**

To this day I still do exercises that look extreme. I power lift. I throw weighted medicine balls 2 miles on a cardio day. I wear a 40 lb weight vest. I sprint as if I have a world competition. I dead lift 500lbs. I train for conflict through martial arts.

I do difficult things because willpower is something which must be exercised. Willpower is weak without constant stress tests. Willpower is not just physical. Willpower is a characteristic of integrity. You need integrity when you are alone and no one is looking. A weak person will always do the wrong thing if it benefits them and they feel no one is looking. You cannot have perseverance if you do not exercise your willpower. Willpower prepares you to push through struggle. People who do not struggle often lack integrity. People without integrity have weak character. If you have good character, it is because strong integrity adheres you to principals. You can only adhere to principals if struggle refines your will power to resist.

Incredibly hard things remind me I can make it through tough times when others quit. If I take it easy when things are good, I can get blind-sided when something challenging happens.

I never create a lifestyle which doesn't hone my willpower. I relax through meditation and playing video games. Relaxing is not the same as taking it easy.

> **Incredibly hard things remind me I can make it through tough times when others quit.**

I tell my body struggle is good.

If the body struggles the mind does too.

My body changed because of past football struggles. I told my body hardship was necessary. I told my body it would succeed despite its physical limitations. I still don't have the same wind strength as a normal person. I blow a 500 on my PSI measurer on a good day.

My 500 PSI lungs can outwork a 950 PSI blow measurer on any given day.

My favorite coach was Pat Lusk. Coach Lusk was a former Marine Recon Ranger. He was the defensive coordinator for Rockledge High School when I attended. The man was the definitions of what the military is suppose to be.

No bureaucracy.

No in between.

No compromise.

No defeat.

The marines have a saying that is popular. I love the saying. The saying goes as follows, "Everyone wants to go heaven but no one wants to die."

Think about the saying for a minute.

Everyone is dreaming about some paradise in the afterlife. Most people dreaming about paradise avoid the passage to paradise like the plague. Many people run away from the thought of death. People do not like bringing up a discussion about death. It's a very interesting concept right? Why do people spend their whole lives dreaming about something they are scared to walk to?

People avoid the struggle which earns them the right to experience their dream.

That is the same with everything in life.

Let's continue with a story I absolutely love. It captures the concept of what I am illustrating in this chapter very well. Bear with me. I promise it will all come together. This story will give you what you need to understand what I describe after this story.

The Story of the Butterfly

On a farm in the Deep South sat a farmer who would tend the fields. Every morning he would toil and make sure he mended his fences. He required the fence maintenance to ensure no animals would get in to eat his crops. One Sunday afternoon the farmer finished tending his fences. The farmer noticed there was a cocoon hanging. The cocoon sat hanging from a fence post near his porch. The farmer approached. The farmer analyzed the cocoon. A small hole in the top of the cocoon had something poking out. The farmer noticed two antennas.

The farmer's face lit up. His daughter loved butterflies! This would be a great opportunity! The father could show his daughter how a beautiful butterfly emerges!

He raced in his house.

"Daughter! Come see this!"

His 5-year-old daughter bolted around the corner.

"Papa what?"

The farmer picked up his daughter.

"Let's go to the porch and I'll show you."

They sat on the porch.

He pointed to the cocoon and told his daughter, "A beautiful butterfly will emerge pay attention."

It was a Sunday. There was no real work to do. So he grabbed his daughter lemonade and himself a coffee.

They sat on the porch and watched. The butterfly poked its head through the hole. Exciting! They both watched intensely. Seconds turned to minutes. Minutes turned to hours. After a few hours they noticed that its head just stayed there. Hmm???? The butterfly's cocoon rattled, shook, and stretched.

Despite all the activity the head of the butterfly never moved.

Despite all the activity the head of the butterfly never moved.

Hours continued. The butterfly kept struggling. Eventually the farmer's daughter fell asleep on the porch. The farmer stared blankly at the cocoon. The butterfly eventually stopped moving.

They had been watching the butterfly half a day.

The farmer felt bad.

This bad feeling wasn't because the daughter hadn't seen the butterfly. What struck a chord with the farmer was the butterfly got stuck. Out of pure exhaustion the butterfly stopped moving.

The farmer became concerned. So the farmer walked over to the Cocoon. The farmer noticed the antennas had gone from upright to pure sag.

The farmer had pity.

The farmer noticed the antennas had gone from upright to pure sag. The Farmer had pity.

The farmer cut a small hole in the Cocoon. He then walked back to the porch. Once the farmer sat down, he noticed the antennas moved back upwards.

The butterfly was ready to move again!

The farmer woke his daughter. He pointed to the Cocoon and she looked.

Slowly the butterfly began to move. Then the head of the butterfly pushed through the Cocoon. Both the farmer and the daughter grew excited.

This was it.

The time for the butterfly to fly had arrived.

Then something surprising happened.

Out emerged a fat caterpillar looking thing with small wings.

What?

The farmer and his daughter walked over to the butterfly. It crawled through the Cocoon on to the fence. The daughter looked at the father and said, "Daddy what's wrong with the butterfly? It looks like a caterpillar with small wings."

The farmer and his daughter never saw the butterfly grow its wings and fly.

The farmer scratched his head. The farmer didn't know. He said, "I don't know baby. Maybe it needs more time."

The farmer picked up the butterfly. He put it in a bucket with grass and other items to nourish it. Maybe it would finish growing its wings after a while. The farmer and his daughter never saw the butterfly grow its wings and fly.

Actually, the butterfly spent the rest of its life crawling around on the ground.

What happened was surprising. It turned out the farmer's haste to spare the butterfly of struggle mortally hurt the butterfly. There was a reason for the unbearably small hole in the Cocoon. The hole was nature's way of making the butterfly push its fluid out from its body.

The butterfly needed to struggle.

The pressure from the butterfly gradually forcing its way through such a small hole would allow the proper allocation of fluid. This proper allocation evenly distributes the fluid amongst its wings. Too much fluid too fast might imbalance the wings. Not enough fluid at the right time would mean the fluid would remain in the body.

> **The butterfly needed to struggle. The farmer's rush to help destroyed the butterfly requirements to fly.**

The butterfly needed to struggle. The farmer's rush to help destroyed the butterfly requirements to fly.

The moral of the story is simple.

You need struggle to be a **Professional Entrepreneur**.

You need struggle to be a **Professional Hustler**.

You can have nothing without watching something gradually happen. There is a reason I say it is typical to see no results for 90 days. Most income will start happening around month 5 (if you are doing it correctly). Until you get to month 9 you are not really doing anything impressive.

Struggle is the building block of willpower.

You must have willpower to go through the uncertainty of not making money.

Cycles of a New Job for a Professional Entrepreneur

I learned an important lesson from struggle early on. The lesson struggle taught me was willpower will form perseverance too. Perseverance is required to survive "Income Cycles". <u>Income Cycles are the natural progression of how a</u> **Professional Entrepreneur & Professional Hustler** <u>earn money.</u> Remember, no one pays your paycheck. You don't get to punch in and punch out as a **Professional Entrepreneur.** No one will worry about making your rent or mortgage payment.

My "Income Cycles" have always followed a similar trend when doing a new deal, project or endeavor.

Make no money for about 60 days.

See some activity around 90 days.

Generate some income around day 120-150.

Earn enough to pay some bills after 6 months.

Watch the income compound and grow around month 9.

Finish the year strong around month 12 with well over 100,000.

This cycle has followed me on every deal I have done in my professional career. Due to this Income Cycle, I have become a "Super Saver". On average, I practice saving about 20-25% of whatever I earn. Remember, entrepreneurs and hustlers are there for "Opportunity" not the "Business". **Professional Entrepreneurs** are like Project Managers.

> **In the Income Cycle process I have become what I call a "Super Saver".**

Project – a temporary endeavor undertaken for a specific purpose with a definitive start and end.

Your opportunity is a project and all projects end.

Save some money.

Let me chronical a live example of how this works. This live example illustrates how the return of my time and money typically exceed gross earnings of 50% per year. In this chapter anything I explain anything I do with money

> **Your opportunity is a project and all projects end.**

(where I allocate my money or a partner's money) must yield over 50% a year to be worth my time. This is not an impossible feat. Making over 50% per year is not a scam. Making over 50% a year on money you invest into an entrepreneurial endeavor is required. I require the aggressive number for the entrepreneurial endeavor because of the risk. Anything slightly better than a coin toss must earn more than it loses when it finally wins. This is called a "Cost Benefit Analysis". Remember income cycles. It is not unusual to starve for 120 days. Your first meal is like a slice of bread on day 121. You are not full from a slice of bread. You don't see a full meal until day 150. You cannot live off something that doesn't properly compensate you for your time. You will fail. You will die. You will not survive. Struggle doesn't mean at the end you have nothing.

That's a fool's quest.

What may shock you is how surprisingly simple, logical and straightforward the process is.

What may also shock you is how **Saturated Markets** will categorize what you do as "dangerous", "irresponsible", or worst "fraudulent".

Remember what you do is not for the common man or woman. What you do is not for a normal person. Normal people get jobs in government. Government jobs provide frameworks of support (pension, vacation, health insurance and job stability). Normal people cannot understand abnormal. The general population does not work like the way I write. What we do is considered abnormal. Donald Trump's 35 day government shutdown in 2019 demonstrated the condition of normal people. The shutdown affected about 800,000 federal employees according to Denise Lu and Anjali Singhvi of the New York Times on 28 January 2019. Nearly 2/3 of them depleted their entire savings within 1 pay check cycle. Think about how dangerous that is. Imagine being part of the 2/3 category of these federal employees. Your family starves after two weeks. That's scary.

What we do is not how the general population works. What we do is not considered normal.

The general population spends all their money to pay bills. The general population participates in an annual savings rate of 2.7% (according to Statista 2017 reports). Most people learn nothing about financial education. When they lose money out of ignorance it is not unusual for them to complain to authorities (regulators). According to an article published by CNN on February 8th 2018 only 17 states require high school students to take a single class on personal finance (not even investing). According to ECampus in an article published by Beth Tallman on October 17th 2017, Tallman informs that of the Americans surveyed 69% of the participants had less than $1,000 in savings. 3% of the Americans surveyed had nothing for emergencies (much less retirement). **Saturated Markets attract**

the participation of these types of individuals. <u>Do not enter Saturated Markets in a creative or unconventional manner.</u>

Remember, I told you this is a high-risk high return game. There are no guarantees. There are only odds. Make sure you play them correctly. A person who has a few thousand dollars can't play in this space. Don't ask them to throw you some money to explore a deal.

I will show you how I played these odds and won.

I will also show you how I played them and lost.

Being Introduced to a True Financial Market Hustle

Towards the end of 2013 I was searching for something more. Financing intermediary service didn't have a long life. As soon as banks opened their doors back open, I would be dead in the water. The money was decent in this market, but my success rate was low. I only saw 2 out of 20 companies make it through underwriting.

For every 10 people who paid me only 1 person went the distance to get funded.

These low odds meant I couldn't charge very high. Low fees with low success meant this service was just a hustle. A hustle which would expire when the conditions of the market shifted.

Immediately following the real estate collapse individuals lost everything. Most people lost their entire net worth. It was not a question of whether an approval came in or not. The central question was "Can you meet the terms and conditions to move to the next stage?"

Typically, the requirement centered on a person having enough liquidity. If you asked for 1mm USD you had to place in escrow a specified amount. The amount ranged from 10% to 25%. Anyone still lending wanted proof people could come up with hard cash. Some wanted escrowed payments in advance. Private lenders wanted people vested in the project's success.

They also wanted to avoid a default.

The truth for my client base was hardly anyone had that much liquidity. My clients strategy was to pay to get a conditional approval. Once they had the approval they would separately capital raise to satisfy the conditions within 30 days.

Many of those borrowers did not meet the conditions.

With most of my compensation being differed on a success basis I weighed the Cost Benefit Analysis.

I was trying too hard to barely gross $100,000 per year. By the time I spent money on plane tickets and hotels I was down to $60,000. This didn't count any referrals. I was lucky if I averaged $5,000 a month for myself net. I needed a change. I needed to find another opportunity.

So in late 2013, I met the CEO of a Forex trading company. I met him through a former real estate broker I previously worked with. This man was the reason I would inevitably end up relocating from Florida to Houston. He was also the reason I did deals in New Zealand. New Zealand is an incredible place. I've seen the highest mountains, the longest deserts, and met some of most genuine people you will ever know. The man who gave me this opportunity was very charismatic. This man could command stage presence. The man was very good at getting himself into deals. I would later discover I mistook this **Businessman** for a **Professional Hustler**.

These individuals are rare breeds. **Professional Hustlers** are individuals who can obtain the minimum credentials required to enter a very "Relaxed Regulated Space". What I mean by a "Relaxed Regulated Space" is – a state, country or territory that permits the conduct of a regulated activity such as investments, insurance, or law not considered developed or stringent in testing actual product knowledge.

> **I would later discover I mistook this Businessman for a Professional Hustler**

A Relaxed Regulated Space market is not a developing market but not quite an emerging market. A Relaxed Regulated Space is a go between. Back in 2013 New Zealand was not known for doing any significant trading, equity exchanges, or foreign currency work. To attract talent from developed markets like the United Kingdom, United States, and China they relaxed restrictions.

As a result, foreign people that sought licensing and registration underwent requirements solely focused on Anti Money Launder (AML), Risk Assessments for Crimes against Fraud, and auditing requirements. Regulators in New Zealand granted exemptions to certain registrants. The registrants had to not be in the business of targeting the host country's citizens. The only barriers registrants overcame were designed to prevent convicted foreign criminals from entering domestic markets.

Obtaining an FBI Background Check with a local law enforcement letter typically satisfied this requirement. The local letters needed to state no pending criminal charges or investigations. Seldom did you get questions about bankruptcy, outstanding judgments or fines (much less bans). Tests on sophistication were not there either. A Relaxed Regulated Space will not have you test to confirm your knowledge – if clients you target meet net high worth requirements and do not live in their country.

Similar exempt New Zealand registrants were required to represent their primary focus was foreigners who fell under high net-worth exemptions. Foreigners had to document their net worth to meet the exemption. There were no product knowledge requirements to test. If a registrant knew requirements to not commit outright crime, knew how to not violate a rule about domestic solicitation and proved the owners were not criminals the registrant was pretty much approved under this exemption.

Things like auditing still needed to be done. The focus of audit was fraud. Auditors wanted to make sure registrants were not foreigners running shops focused on what they called "Mom and Pops". "Mom and Pops" were basically the locals.

Auditors could care less about foreigners; provided they weren't reporting false numbers.

In a relaxed regulation market **Professional Hustlers** thrive. The Hustler can obtain his credentials by learning legal rules for outright crimes, not committing them and then with little to no knowledge (on the actual products) start a business.

There is no crime for being a bad money manager. There is only a crime when you fraudulently represent or mislead someone into thinking something that is not true. This can be a very slippery slope for a Hustler.

In my case, my slippery slope was with US regulators. My slippery slope was the SEC's opinion I did not disclose enough. I informed people I made money from referrals. I did not tell them exactly how much. My opinion was if I did not charge you anything at all, why was it your business to know how much I earned on the back end?

All my clients agreed if I didn't charge them anything they didn't care what I made.

They all signed declarations saying this.

The US regulatory system disagreed with my interpretation; even though it was the opinion of two (2) attorneys I did not violate any law.

It costs money to be right. The biggest financial hurdle in our careers as entrepreneurs is litigation cost. The biggest cost for a hustler is litigation as well. Make sure you count your dollars and pennies for unplanned lawsuits. I could have avoided my civil suit all together with the SEC. I just had to agree to their astronomical number.

I was legally black mailed for fine money. I did not agree with the allegations. I was left with a choice.

Pay to preserve my reputation.

or

Save my money and attempt to explain the allegations aimed to ruin my reputation.

My attorney felt their number was too high.

My attorney felt they were unreasonable.

My attorney felt they did not have their facts straight.

There was a very deep lack of evidence.

My attorney recommended I allow the SEC to file. It would prove out better for me financially. If I just let the chips fall and force them to prove the amounts alleged the lack of proof would be better.

They multiplied my clients by double, multiplied the wire amounts by four, and took an unrelated personal company of my investment advisor clients to help their arguments.

I made a business decision. I decided to take a reputation deduction instead of a financial deduction.

Everything has a cost.

Sometimes you must pay the fare you think is cheaper.

The Hustler can get into a bad situation on accident if the Hustler is not careful. Hustlers sometimes act before they think. Acting before you think is sometimes good but sometimes terrible.

My slippery slope as a **Professional Hustler** cost me. Be careful husting in **Saturated Markets**. It can bite you in ways you wouldn't imagine.

I had no idea my refusal to compromise financially would result in hell bent revenge.

> **The Hustler can get into a bad situation on accident if the Hustler is not careful.**

Sometimes insulting people costs you big. My insult cost me a criminal indictment. Be careful who you embarrass.

Back to the original **Professional Hustler.**

The CEO from my New Zealand company could command a room. The CEO flew down to my close friend's law office. He presented us a presentation. The CEO explained how his "trade" system worked. He modeled the system off a technology my brother would later go on to get patented. He would do this separately with one of the technology's original creators. The patent was a time date stamp technology that eliminated latency in forex transactions. I would help him with this endeavor. This deal would become one of my market wins (the time date stamp company).

During his presentation the CEO showed how with as little as $100,000 he could trade. The CEO showed how his system could make as much as 30% in a single month.

Sound Crazy?

Not really.

I learned how programming could be integrated with a fixed connection. This fixed connection was with a "Prime Broker's" server. A Prime Broker is a custodian who fulfills foreign currency trades. The program's fixed feed in a Prime Broker's server allows an uninterrupted connection. An uninterrupted connection allows trades to fill at a faster rate than standard market accounts. Integrating this connection with cutting edge technology gave the CEO's trade strategy an edge. The CEO also set up his shop as a licensed forex company in New Zealand. In New Zealand this is called a "Financial Services Provider" or "FSP". A company licensed to conduct forex is permitted categorized as an "Introducing Broker". An Introducing Broker is a party that gets paid for making trades on a given account. The beauty behind the CEO's system was the account traded realized compensation as an "Introducing Broker" and a "Client".

In laymen terms, "He was paid a commission trading his own account."

The CEO called these commissions "Rebates". This system was allowed outside the United States. *This is the reason why we conducted all our trades in New Zealand.* Our Prime Broker (known as Al Pari) left the United States when the CFTC rules changed to disallow rebates.

Our Forex Company would place a high degree of trades, via the proprietary algorithm, on the Prime Broker's platform. The proprietary algorithm would manage the degree of "draw down". Draw down is managing losing trades and winning trades to ensure there is a net positive with rebates. We had to work with the Prime Broker extensively. The algorithm needed to match our trade with a liquidity provider (i.e. a 3ʳᵈ party bank). <u>The key was partnering with our Prime Broker.</u> The Prime Broker wanted third parties to fill the order. Trading is a counter party system. One person wins and another loses.

If you go into the system making your Prime Broker losses – the Prime Broker will close your account since it is losing money. It is very important that the person who bets against you not be your partner.

It is very important that the person who bets against you not be your partner.

Let me re-emphasize draw down. Draw down means the amount of equity your account actually "loses" from conducting a trade. The purpose of the algorithm was to perform a high degree of trades. The draw down needed to be manageable. Profitable trades and "Rebates" paid made this happen. As long as the trade was fulfilled by an outside liquidity provider (the bank) the bank was charged the Rebate.

In affect you could lose a high degree of your trades provided the loss was not so substantial that it outweighed your "Rebates".

Let me give you some numbers that will blow your mind.

Nov 2013 –

Current Realized P/L Act. 1 – $(57,477.01)

Current Realized P/L Act. 2 – $(44,267.39)   Total = $(101,744.40)

Commissions –

    Net Deposits Act. 1 $33,415.93

    Net Deposits Act. 2 $33,417.23   Total = $66,833.16

        Profit for Month = $(34,911.24)

Dec 2013 –

Current Realized P/L Act. 1 – $(103,861.94)

Current Realized P/L Act. 2 – $(98,456.71)   Total = $(202,318.65)

Commissions –

    Net Deposits Act. 1 $50,602.82

    Net Deposits Act. 2 $50,536.51

    Net Deposits Misc. $46.02   Total = $101,185.35

          Profit for Month = $(101,133.30)

Jan 2014 –

Current Realized P/L Act. 1 – $(7,365.50)

Current Realized P/L Act. 2 – $(8,018.22)

Current Realized P/L Act. 3 – $(10,462.86)

Current Realized P/L Act. 4 – $(10,464.55)

Current Realized P/L Act. 5 – $(9,167.36)

Current Realized P/L Act. 6 – $(7,118.98)   Total = $(52,594.47)

Commissions –

    Net Deposits Act. 1 $40,742.48

    Net Deposits Act. 2 $0

    Net Deposits Act. 3 $66,941.40

    Net Deposits Act. 4 $13,952.85

    Net Deposits Act. 5 $0.00

    Net Deposits Act. 6 $0.00   Total = $121,636.73

          Profit for Month = $69,042.26

I give you the above ninety days so you can see how these high yield programs actually work. In one month there was a loss of -34,911.24. The following month there was another loss of -101,133.30. That's rough right? It's running in the red about 136,000 at this point. Would you quit?

The next month it records a $69,042.26 profit.

In one month the program made up half the losses it took over 60 days. The program would go on to consistently do about 20% a month thereafter. It was a solid run for the year. We ended the year at around 89% on the money we traded.

> **In one month the program made up half the losses it took over 60 days.**

This system worked well until the Swiss Franc was unpegged from a fixed euro exchange. On January 15th 2014 the Swiss National Bank (SNB) abruptly announced this. We watched as the exchange rate for 1 Franc went from 1.20 euros on a Wednesday to 0.85 on a Thursday.

The SNB announcement caused panic and chaos.

Many hedge funds and prime brokers collapsed.

One of the prime brokers to collapse was Al Pari. Al Pari was our Prime Broker. Our Prime broker went insolvent.

What does insolvent mean?

It means that the Prime Broker holding our money ran into financial issues and had to reorganize due to external issues.

They paid investor money back but considered our commissions forfeited at the end. The Prime Broker owed the Forex Firm nearly 800,000 in commissions the month of the Swiss Franc collapse. Our trader dialed it up on a 1mm USD account. I expressed concern. The market looked volatile at the time. I wasn't confident the Prime Broker could fill trades at a level that high. My advice was to keep the volume low until we could get a handle on a potential SNB announcement. The CEO of the company went against all my advice on the dial up. No one knew the SNB would unpeg the exchange. I thought there might be a new set exchange but not like what they announced.

Regardless, of what we all thought the trade volumes were too many.

The Prime Broker got burned. No Bank picked up the trades. The Prime Broker was stuck honoring our commissions. After the UK Branch went insolvent commissions owed were not prioritized in liquidation. The result was a court wiped out the commission debt to our Forex Company in a bankruptcy administration. Prior to bankruptcy on a 1mm USD account our firm's trader generated about $286,000 in a single month.

These commission on the account successfully paid out.

After Prime Broker insolvency, I left the firm. The CEO changed the business model to project funding. I didn't like the vision. I left project funding for a reason. I don't go one step forward two steps back. I wasn't interested in getting back into that. I left to go start my own US investment advisor firm.

This would end up being a lesson in saturated markets. It was a mistake and a blessing all at the same time. I'll get to that later.

In total, the trader for our Forex firm had 3 negative months. One where he almost lost 35% of the firm's account value. After January 2014 he got into the swing of things. High returns always mean high risk. Don't try something like this if you are not prepared to lose your money. A system like this can work but it can also get caught losing. Nothing is 100%. After the January 2014 drawdown the rest of his months were profitable. Typically, he averaged between 10 – 28% before the CEO's call to dial up the trades.

I want you to understand the point of this story.

There is nothing fraudulent about making over 50% a year. Nothing you read in this example is false. I have the trading records.

There are certain characteristics you must recognize.

Did this have extremely high volatility?

You better believe it.

Is this something risky?

You better believe it.

Can you lose a third of your account value in 30 days?

You better believe it.

Is the risk unmanageable?

Absolutely not.

Should you take someone else's money to do this?

Do so at your own peril.

Think about it. We live in a **Saturated Market.** Pretend you took an everyday person's money to get into this.

How do you think an unsophisticated person would react after losing money in this kind of strategy? Especially when you tell the person it was the goal to make them almost 28% in one month.

Imagine you take his or her last $100,000.

I want you to set aside losing everything the person had for a minute.

Imagine how a person would describe this situation to a regulator in a **Saturated Market**. Remember, regulators in these markets are bureaucrats. Most do not have any real-world experience. These people are career book worms. Most are inexperienced at business or investments.

What do you think the opinion of an inexperienced bureaucrat is on our high yield situation?

Remember these people think anything above 10% a year is risky.

What do you think the opinion is of an inexperienced bureaucrat whose first international transaction is yours?

What do you think your bureaucrat's opinion is when you do not incorporate in the United States?

Think about the facts. You're living in the United States. You and the client are both US Citizens. You are performing the exact same type of service a licensed CFTC representative does...but you are claiming an exemption.

You don't do these activities in the United States.

You run everything in New Zealand, but you live here.

You jump on a plane to go meet your client there but not here.

Now you have a US Citizen complaining about a non-US issue when the other person involved is another US Citizen living down the street.

How does this sound to a layman?

Remember your **Saturated Market** bureaucrat has never gone out the country.

The bureaucrat most likely thinks you are running a Ponzi Scheme. In their mind you registered overseas to avoid detection.

After all a US Citizen doing business with another US Citizen should get licensed.

The question they will pose to themselves is, "Why didn't he or she get licensed?"

Their answer will always be negative in this situation.

They believe there is only one way to do things.

They are programmed to think this way.

Exemption equals dishonesty.

The regulator's approach will be aggressive. The regulator will pose questions which suggest guilt despite the lack of proof. They will say things like, "We are investigating Mr. xx for fraud". They will pause. They will let it sit in. Then they will say "We are not saying Mr. xx has done anything but did you notice anything suspicious?"

Imagine a person listening to a government official say this.

It is going to spook the person.

This person didn't have any suspicion before they sat down with your regulator. Now they don't know what to think.

After all if someone from the government is investigating you it must be bad…right?

In psychology this practice is called Leading Questions.

Regulators on a mission are very good at posing Leading Questions and giving narrations to suggest conclusions.

He/she will smear your name across everyone you know when they question people in this manner. Do you know what prompts a regulator to do this?

Your investor was an everyday joe. Your everyday joe lost their money. Your everyday joe doesn't understand the *Why*. Your everyday joe only understands the *What*. So, your everyday Joe tells the regulators the *What*. The *What* is, "I was promised 20% per month returns, I lost all my money. I don't understand what happened to it. Can you please look into this?"

Can you blame the regulator for doing this?

This is exactly what happened to me in my investment advisor 5 years later. Despite all the records, all the proof it wasn't what they claimed, and the overwhelming evidence contradicting every single statement it came down to…

"You let a few people in that lost everything, These people were not sophisticated

Admitting to nothing costs money. It's all about the money. If it was that bad do you think liberty and justice would be for sale?

people. There was talk of these high returns and we have no idea how you can do that. So, we must do something. We can't go overseas because no one recognizes our authority. You're the only one man enough to actually answer a petition."

So, what happened to me? I was presented an offer by my attorney. Spend a half million dollars in a COVID 19 pandemic to prove they don't know what they're talking about or agree to 1.3mm settlement offer to not admit to any wrong-doing.

When I declined their offer because my attorney could not in good conscious recommend it.

I was served an indictment based on the same civil suit.

Evidence?

None.

Just a lone witness who was in worse shape than me on unrelated matters who lied to save himself.

Admitting to nothing costs money. It's all about money. Liberty and justice are for sale. It is a poor state of affairs. This is the reality of our legal system.

Those 400k salaries for regulatory attorneys don't pay themselves. Especially when there are 4 of them in the room. My olive branch was to pay for a year worth of my reviewer's efforts. Right or wrong I was supposed to cover their pay.

I guess everyone's on a quota.

With everyday joe the best way it ends is agreeing you solicited a person that should not have been there. Your end game is an agreement to neither admit nor deny a violation of some ambiguous section of the Securities Act which no one knew about. The cherry on top is a **huge fine**.

Learn from my mistakes.

Don't get into entrepreneurial endeavors with unsophisticated people. Even if these types of people beg you to let them in don't let them in. Things do not go right in our line of work. When it doesn't go right you are first to be castrated.

Change is hard to accept.

The thing consistent with a **Professional Entrepreneur is change**.

Nothing stays the same.

To a person on the outside it may look like you cannot keep your word. Some people will call you a liar because what you said did not come to pass. Some people will say you don't follow through. Some people will say you are inconsistent. Others will get mad. When you agree to meet someone but need to reschedule due to a pressing matter for money people can feel let down. Keeping your obligations is important but explaining something for the fourth time is very trying.

> **Don't get into entrepreneurial endeavors with unsophisticated people.**

Meeting to say the same thing over and over is sometimes a sign you shouldn't work with someone.

It becomes worse when you email them stuff; they say they read it but are too proud to admit they didn't understand. I stopped taking people seriously because I was frustrated with this cycle.

I sometimes became frustrated. In my frustration I would leave people high and dry. I was tired of disappointment. I was let down time and time again with my expectations. I used it as an excuse to dismiss people. This would come back to bite me. There is no excuse for not following through on what you say.

I am very adamant about doing what I say now.

I am very careful with my words now.

In the past I justified why people like this didn't deserve my time. They continually let me down. Instead of removing them from my circle I kept them involved. I hoped one day they would get it. That was a mistake. My decisions to include certain people caused negative emotions. These emotions aggravated the situation. Don't work with someone if you don't think they can be in the **Professional Entrepreneur** club. It's not their fault. **It's your fault**. If you don't have the time, do not be a false mentor. If you lack the skill to teach don't offer someone to be a student. If someone has no hustle in them don't have them hustle. This field is for people who have certain "talent" and are "wired" different. Not everyone can be what you think they should be. The main enemy of a **Professional Entrepreneur** is ignorance. The main enemy of **Professional Hustlers** is pride.

Ignorant people will never understand you. The only thing ignorant people understand is you told them something should happen. When you tell them a valid explanation for change they don't understand. Lack of understanding leads ignorant people to feel uncertain. Uncertainty can make

> **The main enemy of a Professional Entrepreneur is ignorance**

them feel like you're not a person of your word. It is hard for people to understand a deal relies upon more than just you. It is easier to blame one person than to review the entire situation. Ignorant people always take the easy way out. It's easier to just blame you. So be cautious.

Ignorance breeds fear. Ignorance also breeds assumptions. Ignorance fuels volatile actions. You have no business as a **Professional Entrepreneur** doing business with people who lack financial literacy. Remember this key fact.

Don't force someone to be something you want them to be. That's a form of egoism. You cannot force someone to be something they're not. Forcing people to be something they're not blows back hard. Learn from my mistakes. You shouldn't spend time inspiring a person to be something they're not. People should naturally strive to be in this world. I have never been sued by an entrepreneur or hustler. I have been sued by an investor. The investor type who has always caused me problems was "unaccredited" investors. I have never been sued by an investor who was "accredited" and "sophisticated".

You shouldn't be the only source of a person's learning. Even an amateur should have something to teach you. If a person you're working with never gives you a single unknown fact about what you're both doing they're probably the wrong partner. Most likely they are just riding the gravy train. Cut the trip short and tell them to get off. Everyone likes money. Don't be the guy or gal paying money to learn later the person was just there for the paycheck.

There is something called the 1933 Securities Act. This Act defines people who are "Accredited" and "Unaccredited" Investors. The difference between them is large. An Accredited Investor has a minimum net worth of 1mm USD (excluding his or residence) or makes $200,000 per year for the last two (2) years. If a person is married and the combined household income is $300,000 per year for the last two (2) years – the person can also qualify as an Accredited Investor.

An Unaccredited Investor is basically everyone else.

The rules and exemptions change over the years but this is more or less the idea.

All the trouble from regulators comes from "Unaccredited Investors". Trouble comes for both illegitimate and legitimate deals.

I caution people from attracting investment from Unaccredited Investors. I would probably advise not to do it at all. At minimum you must find a person who is an Accredited Investor to invest. I also recommend you find an Accredited Investor who didn't get there by saving their entire life.

In other words, stay away from the elderly.

There's nothing worse than an old person investing into your endeavor. They always claim elderly abuse if it doesn't work. Legit or not it's best to stay away from the +60 year old age group.

In the securities world there is a standard called "Suitability". Suitability means determining if an investment is suitable or not for a person. Sound difficult? It can be. Anything we discuss in this book is considered "Unsuitable" for an Unaccredited Investor. What we discuss in this book can also be "Unsuitable" for Accredited investors too. Just because a person has money doesn't mean you should take it. Remember I'm trying to teach you from my mistakes.

My goal is to spare you the headache of a civil action from the SEC or worse an indictment.

The general rule of safety is, "An Entrepreneurial Endeavor should accept no more than 10% of an Accredited Investor's Net Worth."

A better approach is, "An Entrepreneurial Endeavor should accept no more than 10% of an Accredited Investor's Liquid Net Worth."

I recommend you find an Accredited Investor who made it as a Businessperson or an Entrepreneur.

Hustlers are rarely Accredited Investors. Hustlers know how to capitalize in a situation to earn money. Hustlers tend to lack skills required to build sustainable models.

Don't get 50-year-old Joe Smith who has a 2mm 401k that spits out 50,000 a year as a result of working for Shell. Don't get Jane Smith who managed to inherit her daddy's company for 30 years managing a "Duh Product". The riskiest thing anyone of these types can do is invest in an Initial Public Offering (IPO). IPOs are surrounded by United States Securities Attorneys. These attorneys will defend any of these individuals' claims.

> **Hustlers know how to capitalize in a situation to earn money. Hustlers tend to lack skills required to build sustainable models.**

When taking money always, I mean ALWAYS, use an attorney. Never take money without something going through an attorney trust account.

Don't take the short cut.

It's not worth it.

Risk is about how you manage the process, analyze the odds, and play them according to an acceptable risk tolerance. The audience you play for is very important. Accept that there are certain instances where you will lose. Just like the typical super bowl team will not win every game – the team will still win the championship.

Sometimes you won't make the championship but you will finish the year with a "Winning Record".

That is how doing entrepreneurial endeavors are.

You need to win more than you lose. How much you win needs to heavily outweigh what you lost. It doesn't matter if you lost 5 times out of 10. If your record is .500 focus on win loss ratios. If you lost 1mm USD on five failed ventures…ensure you gained 4mm on the successful ventures.

Do you know what type of performance this makes?

Under this presumption a net positive performance of 3mm USD are the earnings.

The earnings to loss ratio is a whopping 3:1.

If a person wins three times more in earnings than they lose this is a good thing. Look at the downside too. Let's say a person was involved in a deal which was a complete loss. If this person was involved in the complete loss…that person just lost everything. The issue created with single play opportunities is "Concentration Risk".

Concentration Risk is potentially a big problem.

A person with Concentration Risk is a person who can lose everything. Any person in a complete loss likely doesn't have much good to say about you. Despite your overall record the opinion is most likely bad.

Remember to choose how you involve people in deals. If the only chance of success is a single deal there's a lot of risk. Don't put your best relationships in one off deals.

More important don't take very much money from any one person.

Losing $10,000 is easier to stomach than losing $1,000,000.

The best thing to do is disclose, have a person sign a full waiver (called an indemnification and general release), complete a disclosure section, and then shake your hand. Make sure the person says, "I understand what I am getting into."

If you lack the ability to do this, then I hate to break this to you…you are not cut out for this world.

I always made people sign the strictest documents with the most favorable language. The only time I didn't get the right language accomplished was because I literally "didn't know" the verbiage that should be in there. Good salespeople do not have to "hide" disclosures.

My claims were for "insufficient" disclosure not "non-disclosure".

There is a big difference.

Remember the difference between a "Good **Hustler**" and a "Bad **Hustler**". A Bad *Hustler* makes it a point to *dodge the verbiage* and a **Good Hustler** makes a point to **get it signed** despite the verbiage.

If you do what a Good Hustler does the person might not feel good about how you lost but they should not harbor any ill will against you. You might not do business with the person again. Then again, sometimes people reconsider. People can change their minds if they see you do other successful things.

I've lost people's money before.

I've lost over one million dollars.

It is not a good feeling to lose someone's money but there is risk.

For certain people I've compensated them with interest in separate and unrelated deals. I've personally dug money out of my pocket sometimes. I didn't have to do those things. I gave people interest in my other unrelated stuff because I thought it was the right thing to do. I don't enjoy losing money. I dislike losing someone else's money even more. I feel responsible. Even if legally I don't have any obligation to the person. That's just the way I'm wired. I think that's why people have a tendency to trust me. I'm genuine in that respect.

I do not deny losing money.

I deny stealing money.

We all lose money.

It happens.

Despite bad publicity on search engines, I've had nearly all my relationships stay in my corner. Only two buckled. Both turned due to fear of consequences. Both lied to protect themselves. Both offered to become witnesses against me and serve as the foundation for the allegations in both petitions.

Ironically, the witnesses are not the victims.

Remember there is no crime for losing money. It is why under every investment document any person has ever signed they say the word "risk".

Don't want to lose money?

Don't invest.

Lies always surface. Truth always comes to light. I am not worried. Forgiveness is what helps me move on. When it comes to light what will remain is is their actions.

They must live with themselves.

I can only imagine what it feels like. I imagine them waking up every day. They stare at themselves in the mirror. They know they are there because of a lie.

That is enough punishment for me.

I did everything I said.

My actions will speak.

The people who had true character built me up when others sought to tear me down.

I am fortunate to have people in my corner. This isn't a rant about how I feel. This is a lesson in your future life as a **Professional Hustler** or **Professional Entrepreneur.**

You must invest in character, integrity, and willpower.

When people try to save themselves, shield themselves from lawsuits or avoid money loss consequences they typically misdirect.

Most often you will receive attention from their misdirect attempts.

I am fortunate to have demonstrated my character to certain people. In crucial moments, without looking for fame or notoriety, I showed these people what I did with money. These people witnessed me perform the opposite of the allegations.

Consistently I did the opposite.

Often when I was in worse financial circumstances.

Time and time again I did this with much larger sums.

These people still trust me despite what was alleged for this reason.

So learn from my mistakes on risk management side. Find ways to shield money losses. Take less money. Only take $1.00 out of the $10.00 a person has. That is a responsible way to handle things in this field. Take it a step further with the $1.00 you take.

Did you know you can buy a 30 year US Treasury Zero Coupon with your $1.00 for half the stated face value (i.e. pay $0.50 for a $1.00 US Government Treasury)?

In 30 years it matures to the full face value.

You can take throw the dice with a free conscious if you use a simple strategy like this. The difference between your acquisition price and the face value of the US Treasury is the gamble budget. If you lose the gamble budget, offer your investor the US Treasury. True they can only get half the money now, but every year from now until year 30 it gets closer the face value.

At least you can look them in the eye and say, "It didn't work out, but I didn't lose your money. Here, take this treasury. In 30 years it will be your full value. Right now you can cash out about half if you don't want to wait. Sorry man that's how this goes sometimes."

I don't know about you but that is a much better thing to say than "Hey I lost your money. I'll make it up on the next one." That's never a good line.

If it works out you just got a free retirement. Not too bad huh? (Just make sure you have a proper legal contract to structure the treasury. Otherwise you will get hit for securities violations, unjust enrichment and a host of other problems. Always use an attorney when handling another person's money.)

If you handle people this way, the person has a high chance of doing repeat deals with you. This statement is true even when you fail. If you fail too much the person may say enough is enough and quit on you.

That might happen.

Winning is a habit and so is losing.

Make sure you win more than you lose.

If you keep losing, then maybe you are not a **Professional Entrepreneur**.

You might be a *phenomenal **Hustler***. Or you might be like my New Zealand CEO who was a **Professional Hustler**. Either way, make sure you don't turn an entrepreneurial deal into a business. Worst, never turn a hustle into a business. Both end poorly. Be a <u>Good Hustler</u> not a *Bad Hustler*.

There are many examples of how you can earn over 50% a year on your money. You do not have to do a complicated trade system. I gave you the example above because everyone safeguards the structure. A possible 100%

per annum deal trading is possible. Possible does not mean probable. Make sure you know the difference. I think a trade structure like this shouldn't be a secret. Don't get fooled by high yield returns that are "guaranteed". All of them are derivative of options, forex, or futures. All of them have a high degree of risk. Guarantees can only be used with a Certificate of Deposit, US Treasury or Whole Insurance Product protecting your investment.

Want something simple?

You can double your money by opening up a clothing line, buying it from a wholesale distributor who lets you put your own tags on it, and then sell it for triple the value online. I know a person who is close to me that took $1,000 worth of clothing, branded it themselves, and then collected $4,000 worth of sales.

That's like 300% on your money in 90 days.

Is that a Ponzi Scheme?

No, that's just straightforward business.

Want another example?

Become a supplier for pencils for your local school district. Let's imagine the school district wants pencils at $0.25 per pencil. You realize you can go straight to a Chinese pencil supplier. As long as you buy at least $100,000 worth of Chinese pencils the supplier will give it to you at a price of $0.05. Between your holding costs, interest you promise someone, and shipping you realize it costs you about $0.11 per pencil. You get paid on a net 180 days from the school. You deliver the pencils and wait. You made 100% on your money in about 12 months.

This is a system I've used. I call it a "Prompt Pay System". You then factor the receivable with third parties to survive the one year drought.

You see?

Making a large return is not very complicated.

Making large returns can be simple.

People who call things like this a scam are not businesspeople. It is always easier to decry something than understand it. There is nothing hard about what I described above.

Everything I wrote above is also 100% easy to verify.

When you see tangible examples operating in a straightforward manner it is easy to participate. I have examples like these for days. These are just a few. Hopefully you see why I always talk about a "Cost Benefit Analysis".

Let's analyze the pencil deal again.

Imagine you put the pencil deal together. You took roughly 90 days to gather up the $100,000. Then you took 30 days in a Request for Proposal (RFP) to win the bid. Your order comes in 45 days from China. You deliver it to the school district. You spend 30 days figuring out how to submit your proof for payment.

You wait 6 months from your submission.

You went without money for how long?

Let's add it up. 90-days to figure it out **+** 30 days to go through the bid **+** 45 days for delivery once you confirmed the contract at the end of 30 day period **+** 30 days because you didn't know how to submit a government form **+** 6 months to get paid = 1 Year, 1 Month and 2 weeks.

That's a long time.

It costs you $100,000 direct costs **+** $120,000 indirect for a total cost of $220,000. You were paid $500,000 for a total profit of $280,000. Along the way you needed like $70,000 advanced on your purchase order to survive at some absurd double the investor's money rate (that's what's available for these types of deals). So you cleared a total of $210,000 over about 15 months.

Not a bad living.

That's how **Professional Hustlers** do their high return deals. No scams or Ponzi Schemes involved.

We are just smart out of the box thinkers who are go-getters and know how to *hustle* it in.

If a deal like this goes south and you took someone's money who complains to an authority about some double your money scheme in 6 months…well…now you understand how it can turn into allegations like mine.

So, make sure you're careful with who you involve.

Professional Entrepreneurs can also do these types of deals too.

If you have no track record on the pencil deal you must do something to get it in.

Let's see if you're following me to this chapter's point.

What would you do with no track record?

The point of this chapter is…

You Hustle the money in.

Learning about Red Team Leadership

WHEN I ENLISTED in the United States Air Force Reserves, the first thing they taught me were values. In the Air Force you learn 1) Integrity first, 2) Service before self and 3) Excellence in all we do.

These are core values that have never changed for me.

These core values built my daily convictions. Every day I have reminders on my iPhone go off. I read my convictions every day.

They read,

1. Be without fear in the face of your enemies.
2. Protect the Innocent.
3. Safeguard the Helpless.
4. Do no wrong.
5. Speak the truth even if it leads to your doom.
6. Remember God alone in all you do.

That is your oath.

You attract what you are in this world not what you want. If you have no convictions, it does not matter what you want you won't get it. Write your convictions down. Read them every day. Convictions are not beliefs. Beliefs change. Convictions are values you took the time to research, found evidence of its benefit and convinced yourself to adopt.

Leaders must have conviction.

I have retained a lot of things from the military. Some things I retained from the military include ownership of rifles, marching a few miles a week, training with a knife and a bunch of other things.

Throughout my career as a **Professional Entrepreneur** I learned most people in the business & entrepreneurial world do not have these values.

Often you will read great people tell you about how honesty, hard work, and ethics got them to where they are. It is partially true.

The full truth of the matter is different.

I love Lori Grenier, Beyonce, Bill Gates, Warren Buffet, Sara Blakey, Gary Vaynerchuck, and Mark Zuckerberg. The people I named are the pinnacles of the entrepreneur weight class. Individuals who preach the best way to be are the apex of the pyramid.

What I am teaching you is different. Remember I am about probability not possibility.

The goal is for you to consistently earn $100,000 a year.

My book is like an associate degree.

I am going to teach you how to 1. Elevate your financial status, 2. Earn money unconventionally, and 3. Have a career which has at least a 75% chance of being a millionaire over 10-15 years.

My methods also require patience. There is no overnight success story with me. Nothing happens overnight but everything happens all at once.

I am the equivalent to being a Titan in the World of Greek gods. Titans are powerful. Titans can even fight the Greek gods. Titans often lose in all-out war with Greek gods. Being a Titan is not a bad thing though.

I am a Titan not a Greek god.

Remember who is giving you advice.

A Titan could defeat a Greek god in a unique and special circumstance. If this happened I would say this feat would be the upset of the century. Don't get over confident. Don't be a small Titan openly confronting a Greek god.

You will be crushed.

Businessmen and **Businesswomen** are still much savvier than a **Professional Entrepreneur.**

There are 328,467,873 people in the United States per the United States Census Bureau Clock (as of 2/20/2019 611PM Central Standard

Time). With the total population in mind I want you to review some very interesting statistics.

In a single quarter in 2016 they reported it that 240,000 establishments started up according to the Small Business Administration Small Business Profile 2018.

The Small Business Administration Business Profile 2018 covered these other statistics:

- Small Businesses that held 1-499 Employees totaled 5,881,267
- Small Businesses that were very similar to businesses I have worked with totaled 5,265,682 (1-20 employees).
- Businesses that had no employees at all totaled 24,331,403 (A **Entrepreneur** & *Hustler* dominated category).
- The total small firms available that were "registered" and doing "actual" business in the United States were 30,212,670.

If you are led to believe that all the people above are honest, hard working, considerate human beings you are in for a surprise.

Most of these people are not.

Most people in business are what I call "amoral".

Do you know what amoral is?

Per the Merriam-Webster Dictionary *Amoral* is defined as

1. Having or showing no concern about whether behavior is morally right or wrong.
   a. Being neither moral nor immoral.
   b. *Specifically*: lying outside the sphere to which moral judgments apply.
2. Being outside or beyond the moral order or a particular code of morals.

Now I know anyone that is arguing with this is saying

"I know a hundred people that are not like that when I do business."

The point is *you know* a 100 people. <u>There are almost 29 million</u>. *You don't know everyone* and your limited sphere of influence is not all there is.

We often associate our reality with reality.

That is form of ego...get rid of it.

Your life is not the same.

As a **Professional Hustler** I estimate cycling through at least 10,000 of these people in my past 14 years.

Some were so disorganized I passed. I could not even figure out the structure of an SPV with disorganized business owners. Some people rubbed me the wrong way (doing things like lines of drugs in front of me at a bar). Many broke their words openly despite shaking my hand and looking me straight in the eye on simple things. I don't do deals with people like that. In my deals I only talked about the major deals. Major deals are transactions where I invested at least 75% of my time on that one thing. There were a lot of "paid favors" I did over my career. These paid favors were simply one-off projects. Many amounted to nothing more than a few thousand dollars of earnings to my pocket.

Trust me I've worked with a lot of business owners. I've worked with many people who thought they were business owners too.

The real question you often hear from this group of business individuals are,

"Is it legal if I do this?"

See Business People, Hustlers, and Entrepreneurs alike are concerned with staying within the confines of the law. I would say 9 out of 10 of them are not interested in going to jail.

It absolutely shocked me when I was indicted.

Trust me it never once came up in my mind to cross the law.

I never imagined bank wire fraud could be so broad.

Did you know you can be charged for bank wire fraud even if you didn't benefit from the money, didn't know where it went, got deceived of its purpose and realized zero economic benefit from it?

The law is tricky.

Now you know why I say always use an attorney.

I believe amoral behavior of business owners and government officials are the reason the United States is ranked the most litigious jurisdiction in the world. Non criminal activities can still result in "civil" lawsuits.

According to a chart published by eLocalLawyers on September 7th 2011, 80% of the world's lawyers live in the United States.

In 2010 alone, they spent $1.6 billion **on settling frivolous lawsuits outside of court** according to eLocalLawyers. I settled a previous claim in Oregon although I felt it was frivolous. Because of frivolous lawsuit settlements they took a survey that found just 16% of people in business stated they trusted the legal system to protect them from frivolous lawsuits (eLocalLawyers 2011).

Remember the biggest hurdle of a **Professional Entrepreneur?**

I called it the "Legal System" – make sure you remember that.

Most lawsuits that successfully award money comes from are suits against organizations (i.e. businesses).

Let's continue on some interesting statistics on individual file suits (Plaintiff wins 55% of all tort trials in the United States according to eLocalLawyers 2018):

1. 11,224 lawsuits – Individual vs. Individual : Plaintiff Awards $20,000 per case

2. 7,472 lawsuits – Individual vs. Business : Plaintiff Awards $80,000 per case (Remember my Oregon settlement? The payment was about this much way to be a statistic)

3. 1,546 lawsuits – Individual vs. Government: Plaintiff Awards $80,000 per case (Man I have my fingers crossed on this one)

4. 1,393 lawsuits – Individual vs. Hospitals: Plaintiff Awards $600,000 per case

Less than 15 cents of every dollar for the cost of a tort goes to compensation for the litigant. <u>Attorneys are eating up most of the award money</u>. This is why I say, "Attorneys can crush it as an Entrepreneur". Hopefully you understand why I say, "If I could do it all over again, I would be an attorney."

In general, most people in this industry avoid blatant fraud.

Remember, I wasn't charged with securities fraud or defrauding investors. I was charged with bank wire fraud – a very broad, tricky and technical method of hemming someone up.

All it takes do conduct bank wire fraud is write transfer instead of purchase on a wire slip and you've potentially defrauded the bank.

Many leaders of business organizations have an adaptable moral code. This code shifts based on who they are speaking to. This flexible moral code also adjusts for the person who will procure them money. Typically, most business organization leaders compromise their personal beliefs to earn a living.

We all have heard the cliché, "It's just business, it's nothing personal."

Now you might say.

"Chris if you are saying the majority are amoral, how did you work with all these people?"

This is a great question. Let me give you more questions to illustrate how I will answer you.

How do you work with someone that wants to bond with you in an activity you see as deplorable?

How do you work with someone who has questionable personal behaviors and needs?

How do you get to know someone you don't like outside of the office?

How do you get into bed with someone (businesswise) that will adopt lifestyles you do not approve of?

How do you work with a business whose leaders will compromise personal beliefs?

Make these amoral bastards conform to your opportunity.

This sounds very challenging doesn't it? Think about it. Wal-Mart lets anyone walk through their doors and buy their products. If Wal-Mart was concerned with only transacting business with moral people they would find screening procedures to prevent criminals from buying groceries. Wal-Mart is also one of the largest contributors to "Habitat to Humanity". Interesting isn't it?

If CVS didn't approve of customer drug abuse, they would profile people who show symptoms of tobacco abuse. I bet you are thinking "What did you say?"

No one in CVS or Wal-Mart enforces moral screening though.

What does that make the people who lead these organizations? Are these people bad people?

I am not saying people who do not enforce moral standards are bad.

It goes back to the concept of "amoral".

I also want you to understand something about "Stereotypes".

In my view, Stereotypes are about 60% accurate. In a Stereotype label enough people do what the Stereotype identifies but there is a significant portion of the group who do not. If you are ignorant and say all people are like your Stereotype – you are doing a huge disservice to anyone in their group. Don't be an idiot. Not all Mexican business owners in Southern California are contractors. You will insult the owner of a Mexican American owned financial services firm if you ask him where his flooring guys are. At the same time you will find Mexican Americans dominate the construction work in Southern California. Which is it?

In general, I recommend you have a predisposition on what to expect with a Stereotype but do not jump to conclusions. I recommend you wait to treat someone the way the Stereotype describes unless the person acts the way the Stereotype categorizes. Have your guard up but don't penalize the person. Give the person the benefit of the doubt that the person you are working with is the exception.

If not, the signs will show.

A sign would be the prospective partner tells you one thing and writes in a contract the complete opposite. When you confront the prospect, the person will state, "My attorney drafted it for legal reasons. I will get it changed."

Generally, most people have no concern about whether behavior is morally right or wrong in this space. Most people only care if it is legal or illegal.

If someone is acting lawfully immoral – the typical **Businessman / Businesswoman** will not care.

This indifferent behavior hits at the core of why I always say what I am about to say.

I am there for the "opportunity" not the "business".

If there is an opportunity for you to legally benefit through someone else's business, I call that "Clearance to Act". I view every business that has an opportunity for me as a "Special Purpose Vehicle" (SPV).

A Special Purpose Vehicle (SPV) is a legally organized entity utilized to procure income on a specific project or transaction.

I am not concerned with who or what the businesspeople are. What I am concerned with is maintaining my integrity to accomplish my specific goal. I can force anyone to act in a moral way to accomplish one task they want to benefit from. The motivation is money for the normal **Businessman** or **Businesswoman**. That is how amoral people conform to your opportunity. Amoral **Businessmen / Businesswomen** conform to other things why not a reason to make money with you?

My motivation is my integrity.

The risk to you when working with amoral people is they may do shady things away from you. The consequences can be as little as reputation damage. Sometimes they can be as high as an indictment.

My only regret is not distinguishing between people with sketchy histories.

If someone was willing to do legitimate ethical transactions I typically didn't care about their history.

I judged them on their treatment of me not others.

This allowed me to be manipulated.

This was a failure in judgment on my part. Learn from my mistakes. Do research on a person's history. Just because they are willing to do the "right thing" with you doesn't mean they are doing the "right thing" away from you.

It is possible to get dragged into unrelated matters because of this.

Leading people like this can be tricky.

In the military we have a concept called a "Red Team".

The only Leadership I know how to teach really well is managing "Red Team Members". My leadership style focuses on how you manage an elite group of performers. These elite performers are interested in excelling under an SPV situation. These individuals are highly talented, strongly independent and have a hard time conforming to a rigid structure.

Red Team members do not listen well.

Red Team members perform outstanding.

Red Team members have a hard time being told to adhere to an organized structure.

The lack of participation and adherence to an organized structure results from an extreme disorder called "Talent" with Red Team Members.

In the military the Red Team is a specialized unit. All members typically possess the same or comparable rank. They deploy the unit into a hostile setting to accomplish a single specific task. The task is set according to their unique skill set.

I lead Red Teams.

If you are looking to manage these types of people, I can teach you this effectively.

If you are looking to join a culture where you will become entrenched in the organization permanently you need some other guidance. I would encourage you to pick up a book from a successful **Businessman / Businesswoman** that has built a great brand. A person I think really gets today's market is Gary Vaynerchuck. He is progressive. Gary understands how yesterday's concepts are important today but may be irrelevant tomorrow.

Gary has an interesting style I commend. Gary is walking the talk in a very evident way. Gary has great insight into how you need to be in business today.

Lori Grenier is someone I admire tremendously. Lori took one idea and turned it into a multi-million dollar international brand of well over 700 products. This woman is one of the most understated, under celebrated entrepreneurs of our age. If you do not know who this woman is stop reading and go look her up on Google.

It's important you recognize some principals stay consistent no matter what age you are living in.

A principal which is consistent through the ages, "You don't get loyalty by betraying people."

Certain things are common sense.

Some things like doing all your marketing through a phone book may single-handedly sink your business. This would be an example of an outdated strategy from a marketing expert in the 1980's.

Doing road team tours in time share sales is an example of how something that worked in 2000 sunk my company in the late 2010's. I took outdated business advice from old stars that fell from heaven a long time ago. I should have seen these people as meteors not shooting stars.

Red Team Leadership Principles

Fiercely independent creatures have a hard time fitting in. A good example of a group that can survive alone but choose to work together is a wolf pack.

Have you ever heard the saying, "He's a lone wolf?"

Wolves can survive alone or survive together.

It is possible for wolves to thrive in a pack. Sometimes pack members leave and come back later.

I organize Red Teams just like a wolf pack.

In a Red Team there is a "Pack Leader" and a "Pack Member".

Wolves are very peculiar creatures. In a wolf pack the wolf leader stays "behind" in a march. As humans, we are use to leaders leading from the front. This can be a hard concept to learn.

What the leader of the pack does is organize. The wolf pack leader will put the sick and old at the front to set the pace. The strongest members trail behind the sick and old. The strongest members are there to defend the old and sick. Then the individuals in the middle represent your normal members (strong, healthy, talented and able). The flank of the wolf pack is always protected by elite members of the pack as well. In the way that the leader organizes the march the strong have to work together. The best work together on a march to protect parts of the pack which have equal importance.

Guess who trails the end?

The wolf pack leader.

The wolf pack leader makes sure they leave no one behind.

Refusing to leave a member of your pack behind "through action" is a very important point.

This simple analogy illustrates how you must lead your Red Team Members in entrepreneurial ventures.

Each individual comes together for the "hunt". The "game" is the "deal". The pursuit of closing the "deal" is the "hunt". The individuals of your Red Team Pack will go where you as the leader direct them because of certain knowledge. The knowledge your Red Team Pack Members know is if they get "hurt" or are "too sick" to continue on the "hunt" the leader won't abandon them.

Given the unique situation of so many independent people working together the thing some say each Red Team Member lacks is "third party loyalty". Remember your "members" are not "employees". Your members do not earn a paycheck. Your members must "kill" what they "eat". Therefore if they get "sick" your members are use to being left behind with no scrap saved for them.

No one usually saves an entrepreneur / business person a piece of the deal they do not see to closing. People act this way towards entrepreneurs because of what I call an "Us or Them syndrome". People typically say, "You are either with us or with them". This simple syndrome goes beyond race, religion or creed. Christians fight with each other and so do Muslims. Democracies can wage war against each other (remember the US Civil War). Each entrepreneur is so unconventional the entrepreneur rarely fits well in someone else's box. Therefore, people tend to categorize your members as a "Them". What appears to be "insubordination" with a Red Team member is usually why they are ousted wherever they go.

The member doesn't understand how to inspire loyalty outside their sphere of influence. They usually limit the sphere to whatever culture they lead and create.

An example of a limited sphere of loyalty would be if a member of your Red Team is the CEO of their own company. The member's employees are loyal to them if they are the business owner. The issue with Red Team Members is they are usually the reason "why" they make money. No one around them will generate money for them. So their loyalty is an illusion. Their employees will not band together to pay their rent. The loyalty a Red Team Member has at their company is limited to putting a bunch of money in everyone else's hand. I know tons of entrepreneurs who have spheres like this.

The member you often have is extremely talented but lacks many skills.

When a member of a Red Team meets someone who "allows" them to "create" in any manner they want – they become very loyal.

When they see the Red Team Leader will pick up after them and get their back in a tough financial situation – loyalty is hardened.

This is how you get people who march to their own beat to march to yours. Now remember, you cannot tell people who are entrepreneurs to do exactly as you say. You cannot tell them, "Do it exactly this way."

Tell them, "I need this goal accomplished and you must come through for me. I need you to do what you know how to do and deliver. If you do what I know you can do, we will reach this point. I always have your back. Now I need you to get mine."

That's how you inspire leadership in a Red Team. You must be a wolf pack leader. Know the sick and elderly already know exactly where to go. You don't need to tell the seniors how to pick the right route to the top of a mountain. The seniors climb it the best way already.

As a wolf pack leader you are a "facilitator" on a path rarely walked.

You must point out things. If you see something the person is doing wrong intervene. Your intervention cannot be disruptive. Your intervention must be conducted in a way where the lead sees their actions are not delivering the results "they want" (not what you want).

Your intervention must be a method your member recognizes as a safeguard against the member being left behind.

You must always come from a position of concern, thoughtfulness, and **desire to do the best for them.**

No smart Red Team Member will fight you when your concern is only for their wellbeing.

Your concern for their wellbeing makes sure everyone achieves their goal. You both want to close the deal. There will be no argument on that point. Therefore, pointing out prudent observations you gain from "walking in the rear" allows you to get a "wider prospective".

As a pack leader you don't care how the "game" is "killed". Pack leaders want a "hunt" to result in a "kill".

The members at the front of the march appreciate this view.

A safety in football sees the "entire field". Your members on the front line will appreciate you can see it's a pass play (when they are busy down in a four point stance).

As the captain you can call an auditable. Your front-line members won't just shoot a gap blindly. Trust me they will appreciate your audibles.

As a Red Team Leader you must explain everything.

It's not like commanding **Employees** who do what they are told.

Red Team Members need to understand what you are talking about.

Red Team Leaders master *"patience"*.

If you lack patience you will never put together a bunch of people who think they are all leaders to work towards a common goal.

It is impossible.

Your leadership method must be like changing the direction of a river. The river flows "one" direction. You are the ebb in the shore banks that gradually diverts the river. You never stop the river from flowing. Eventually you can ebb so far, the river is going Southwest instead of Southeast.

You will notice the river still goes "south".

That's because the river will only ever go "south". You can alter how it goes "south" but the river will always go "south".

The river analogy is like managing Red Team Members. Red Team Members are always "independent". You can influence the "independence" of your Red Team Members actions. You cannot remove "independence" from your Red Team Members.

The parties you bring together in a Special Purpose Vehicle (SPV) are all leaders of their own entities. Therefore each entity will file its own taxes, run its own books, set its own policies, and conduct its own culture.

I want to sum up what I've taught you so far in a concise message:

As a **Professional Entrepreneur or Hustler** who is the "leader" you are the leader of a Red Team – a unit organized (as an SPV) for a highly specialized purpose (i.e. your opportunity) that requires the participation of team members (your wolf pack) whom you must lead (the Professional Entrepreneur) on a temporary endeavor (project) that has a definitive start and end (you closing your deal and getting paid) that surfaced because of certain conditions (disorganization, personal reasons or an emerging concept).

Make sense?

I hope it does. I crammed well over 100 pages into a short, concise message. I have to teach you more things before I am done.

Try to keep up young wolf.

Characteristics
of a Professional
Entrepreneur & Hustler

PEOPLE UNDERESTIMATE THE importance of knowing themselves. To become a **Professional Entrepreneur or Professional Hustler** you must have certain characteristics. I learned something very interesting from a man named Tai Lopez (no relationship). This man stated the most successful people in the world excel in certain categories according to the HEXACO Personality Inventory Test.

The test is a measure of the six major dimensions of personality. The test was published by two researchers in 2009. Dr. Kibeom Lee and Dr. Michael C Ashton began the research of the approach in the year 2000. The HEXACO Personality Inventory Test is highly cited and referenced. They consider it the most accurate test currently available by several psychology experts. It was developed as further discoveries in psychology designed to replace the previous models. The test has had many notable achievers test.

I would encourage you to take this test online at hexaco.org to determine where your behavioral traits are.

What the HEXACO PI Test has found in common is that successful entrepreneurs and business people score extremely high in the areas of Conscientiousness.

Conscientiousness comprises the following areas:

1) Organization
2) Diligence
3) Perfectionism
4) Prudence

My personal scores were 4.75 Organization, 5.00 Diligence, 4.75 Perfectionism, and 4.50 Prudence.

The scores are modeled on a 1.0 – 5.0 range. They use the range of the score to determine if you are in the 10th percentile all the way to the 90th percentile. What this means is if you are say a 5.0, the average sample range is 2.88 – 4.71, than you are a higher score than 99.9% of everyone.

Before you get all happy about getting a higher score than everyone else you need to understand a high score isn't a measure of achievement. All the range tells you is that you are on "One End of the Spectrum".

That's it.

SO when you see a high or low score you must correlate it with what type of behavior pattern you have in the category.

You may want an extremely low score in one area and an extremely high score in another.

I scored a 1.00 on Dependence and Fearfulness. The average range in that category was 1.88 – 4.00 for Fearfulness and 2.00 – 4.25 for Dependence. That means that 99.99% of everyone exhibited behaviors that would either 1) prevent them from doing something that they were scared of or 2) require some form of emotional support to vent about during hard times.

I require neither anyone to tell me it will be okay nor do I require anyone for me to talk to about my problems.

I told you before. I am extreme. I am not saying that is a good or bad thing. I'm just wired like that.

Having no fear can be viewed as "reckless" if the person has no "prudence". Not showing any "affection" combined without seeking "affection" could possibly be a recipe for "depression".

I once had a partner who was one of the most special women in the world to me. I think because of her, I developed a behavior high on Altruism (4.00) where the range is 3.00 -4.63.

Generally, I will not do something if I think it will hurt someone deeply. I have come to the conviction you cannot become a lifelong partner with anyone if you do not consider how your behaviors will affect the person.

I am a 4.00 on Fairness which means being fair is important to me. I have a saying. The saying goes like this,

"I don't know if everyone will call me fair. What I know is the concept that keeps me up at night when I'm deciding is being fair."

I would encourage you to have the same thoughts. According to self reported statistical sources with HEXACO the most successful people in life (the top 1%) score high scores in Conscientiousness.

I count myself a "**Professional**". I am a **Professional Hustler** not a **Businessman.** I would not even call myself an **Entrepreneur.** I have entrepreneurial characteristics but that alone doesn't make me an **Entrepreneur.** I rank my *profession* against other *professions.* These professions consist of other people such as doctors, lawyers, accountants, engineers, et cetera.

Let's talk about what it takes to be in the top 1% from a **Professional Hustler** prospective. As a **Professional Hustler,** you are selecting a "*profession*". If you become a **Professional Hustler** you are not opening up a "business". As a **Professional Hustler** you may incorporate your activities for tax or legal reasons. That is okay. That is what I do. Since the only real mark of a "*profession*" is how much it earns that is how we identify how being a **Professional Hustler** compares to other "*professions*". The income earners that make up the top 1% of American Households based on 2015 income tax data (the most recent available year I could find) are as follows:

The top 1% of taxpayers nationally makes an annual income of $480,930. The top 10% of taxpayers make at least $138,031.

So if you are measuring yourself (as I do) on how much money you are making (through your personal or personal company bank account) compared to every other profession (Doctors, Lawyers, Surgeons, Accountants, Engineers, et cetera) do something simple. Look at what other professions are making and look at what the American Households are reporting.

To excel as a **Professional Hustler** all you need to do is earn at least $138,031 to be a better scorer than 90% of your competition.

That's it.

If you want to enter the realm of Titans you need to gross through your personal entity (where you are the only one entitled to ownership) at least $480,930. **Professional Hustlers** corporate entities are not really businesses. It is unfair to lump incorporated hustlers in with incorporated businesses. What **Professional Hustlers** do is organize corporate entities for tax purposes and legal protection. The organization of incorporation is done strictly to take advantage of distinct temporary opportunities.

That is what I do.

Do you want to hear what my performance record showed each year up to 2021?

Here it goes (Gross Earnings): $238,106 (2015) to $342,317.06 (2016) to $462,300.57 (2017) to $568,819.61 (2018) down to $115,795.00 (2019) and a slight increase to $215,121.00 (2020).

2019 was the year of my bankruptcy, SEC investigation, biotech company ouster and divorce.

2020 was the year of the COVID-19 outbreak.

Both were very rough years on me. These performance numbers illustrate how much income can swing in our profession.

Professional Hustlers offer services that benefit an "entire" business. We also refuse being employed because we define our own worth.

So in 2018, I made it to the 1% weight class. I missed it in 2017 by less than $18,000. In 2017 I was probably the top 1.02%. From 2006 to 2010, I always ran among Titans. During COVID, bankruptcy and divorce I still managed to eek out pretty good earnings.

2021 will be known as the year of my indictment and SEC civil case. I'm not done with my earnings this year, but they aren't bad.

Winning is not a sometimes thing it's an all the time thing.

Remember, I said I was a Titan?

How much does Floyd Maywheather Junior earn per fight? How about Lebron James per season? All these people are part of the 1%. Once you make it to the 1% you are allegorically in the realm of the Greek gods. If you barely get in (like me) you are just a Titan.

Anyone of those people I challenge could crush me. I cannot compete with people on their level. I can compete with many people. I can outperform most. I just cannot outperform everyone. A Titan can ascend to heaven…but you have to "ascend".

I once heard an interview about Mitt Romney on CNN. The person being interviewed was Newt Gingrich. Newt was asked during the 2012 race what he thought about Mitt's failure to disclose his tax returns with Bane Capital.

Newt said something I will never forget.

"The thing about Mitt was he was a guy that chased deals. Mitt chased deals for over 8 years. Then one day he closed it. That's Mitt."

Mitt Romney sounds like a Titan that finally cracked one.

Remember, you don't really have a business as a **Professional Hustler**. As a **Professional Hustler** you have a talent that is so unique and riveting that others will build a "business" around you.

Sometimes it is the same for entrepreneurs.

World-class athletes, actors, writers, comedians, or body builders are examples of raw uncut entrepreneurs and hustlers. These individuals propel a unique behavior that can be riveting. Others build business models around people like this.

An example would be a movie production studio that only focuses on "A" list celebrities.

Another example would be a publishing house that only looks for New York Times Best Sellers to distribute.

Get the meaning?

The **Professional Hustler** I was in the past is unique. This **Professional Hustler** does not attain the attraction of fame. An example of this elusive category would be running into someone who does well for themselves; however when you ask a simple question, you don't understand the answer the person gave you.

The question is, "So what do you do for a living?"

The **Professional Hustler** talented in identifying opportunities within markets (that businesses participate in) will proceed to talk about a lot of things. There will be no one answer. Often this type of **Professional Hustler** will talk about everything from his real estate project in Costa Rica to the book deal he is working on with a leading author. At the end of the conversation most people will walk away saying, "I don't know what that person does. I think that person is an investor or something."

The job of the **Professional Hustler** in this "Deal Class" is it to identify opportunities. The opportunities that the **Professional Hustler** identifies allow their "talent" to "earn" income for him / her.

As a **Professional Hustler** I have a keen eye for getting into deals and putting together transactions that result in "earned income" to me. What I am involved in will change by the year. I can be in real estate construction one year, then manufacturing the year after and maybe after 2 years I will be doing scientific research.

A **Professional Hustler** finds the industry that has an "opportunity" and rides it until the market changes it.

Obviously if I took all my earnings into my personal account taxes would murder me. Prudent practices mean I control what goes to me personally and what is allocated through my corporate entity. I set up an LLC, a Corporation or just a Partnership depending on my expected income for the year.

Remember **Professional Hustlers** are not **Employees**. So we do not get paid like them.

Businesses organized as incorporated entities have real products, services, or technologies *catered towards consumers*. When consumers change the **Businessman** or **Businesswoman** works hard to build their "brand" so the consumer accepts the change of product.

An example of a **Businessman** who knows how to be an Entrepreneur would be Jeff Bezos of Amazon. Amazon started off as an online shopping platform. Now Amazon does web hosting services. Amazon also has a trucking delivery company. Now Amazon is going into production and entertainment. What is Amazon? Amazon is a business founded by an Entrepreneur who knows how to adjust with his market to cater towards his consumers. This situation is an example of a unique skill set that only a Business Person has. This book is not about business.

This book is about being a **Professional Hustler** who sometimes is a **Professional Entrepreneur** (not always).

Remember that.

A **Professional Entrepreneur** is always a hustler, but a **Professional Hustler** is not always an entrepreneur.

The consumers of a business can be corporate (B2B) or individuals (B2C). Businesses are manufacturers of tools, marketing agents with multiple employees doing promotional work, or engineers who win contracts to subcontract an entire project out from a major corporate supplier (in lieu of hiring employees).

Remember what it is to be **Professional Hustler** or **Professional Hustler.** Differentiate the difference of a **Businessman / Businesswoman**.

You can lose real big if you scale your opportunity into a business.

Any project I do I look at where I stand at the end. I always look where I stand on the playing field every upcoming year too. I might need to change sports.

Just because my performance is not as high as others in my weight class I do not get down. I remember something. I remember I am achieving more than 90-99% our United States Population.

My skill set is not limited to one business or one service.

I am a survivor.

I am the 1%.

I'm a damn good **Professional.**

I stand at the gates for the elite with my badge accepted. I will not allow anyone not part of this club get me down. People will hurl insults at me despite Instagram not tagging me for "most successful guy alive".

People will say negative things about me. They will find information in a google search engine I was indicted, investigated by the authorities, arrested at one time, or sued by the SEC.

It does not matter.

The only thing you can control when things are bad is your attitude.

All you can be is authentic and transparent.

It is not your job to be liked by everyone.

Elon Musk was charged with securities fraud.

Elon Musk is still running Tesla.

I will not allow anyone get me down for not recognizing who I am when I walk.

I will not allow anyone get me down for saying I am not the type of person to associate with.

Take whatever negativity in your life is weighing you down and use it to build yourself up.

Sun Tzu said famously, "In the midst of chaos, there is also opportunity."

I will find my opportunity in the midst of today's chaos.

You need to be the same.

Find opportunity.

This path in life is not a competition for fame or glory.

This path in life is not for popularity.

This path in life is not for the weak.

As a **Professional**, you *"compete"* against other **Professionals**. Your report card is what you file on taxes.

If someone making less than you is poking fun at you, the joke's on them.

If you are doing well at this, then you are excelling in your bottom line. If you are not doing well at this profession, you will know quickly.

Remember Cost Benefit Analysis?

Make sure time you allocate towards something is worth your time. If not, you may have to find a different profession.

Let's look at some character traits of successful people a bit more. When I say successful people, I don't mean people who are rich. I mean people who apply their minds to something and accomplish it.

In this instance we are trying to win at earning money. In another field you might be trying to win a sports game (literally). So the sports game profession is not about money. It's about performance.

Any performer has characteristics that allow them organization.

Illustrating Organization

In early 2007 I watched Mark Cuban give an interview on ESPN. During this time, I was just getting going. This would be my first successful entrepreneurial venture (Real Estate and Mortgage Company). Until the point I watched Mark make his comment I had earned somewhere around $400,000. My brother and I were enjoying our first taste of success. I still had nearly 5mm to go in gross earnings. What would optimize my performance was something simple. Mark made a very simple statement.

Mark Cuban said he wrote everything he ever did on a notepad to reach his first great championship. Mark said he literally wrote every important call, conversation or item they required him to do that day. Mark said he beats everyone else because of how organized he is. I thought about that statement.

Mark's statement struck a chord with me.

I was organized enough to write a business plan, document strategies for houses, but not organized enough to write what I had to do for the day? From that point on I wrote everything I would do for the week. I didn't use a notepad because I had a computer. I used something simple called Microsoft Word. There are more effective scheduling applications in the market today. I still use Microsoft Word. I use Microsoft Word because it reminds me of writing. When I am in a meeting, I write down notes because it helps me remember. Something about the manual process helps me retain information. That is why I still practice what may seem like an archaic habit today. I can speak my schedule into Siri but I will forget it. When I write it down, I remember it.

From that day on I became a super organizer.

I can tell you exactly what I was doing at the beginning of this decade to the day. I am talking about to the day I am writing this statement. I am talking about a random Monday. I am talking about February 22nd 2010. Don't believe me? I will list what I did nine years ago right now:

February 22nd 2010 Monday

1. Email Account Log in Set Up SED (x8)
2. Executed Contracts Knight Merchant Banking
3. Complete Zip Assembly Knight Merchant Banking
4. CFO briefing on Merchant Account Set Up **(Name Omitted for Privacy)**
5. Bank of America Delivery of Merchant Account Contract
6. **(Investor Name Omitted for Privacy) follow up conversation for 250k (**postponed until tomorrow)
7. Director Email of Knight Merchant Banking Package
8. Preliminary Questionnaire Report
9. Agreement for Pay Structure for Merchant
10. **(Name Omitted for Privacy)**Addendum US Financial Assist LLC
11. **(Name Omitted for Privacy)** formal pass down project assignment
12. Press Release (KI)
13. Director Solicitation

Can you tell me right now what you were doing nine years ago to the day? Can you tell me if I ask you exactly what you did on a Monday five years ago?

Can you tell me how you organized your priorities four weeks ago and what priorities you put in place?

I can.

You see Organization is a characteristic embedded within every successful person. There is no champion in any field that says, "I just arrived here one day without a plan."

For a champion there has to be a plan.

For a champion there must be a systematic way of modeling your behavior.

For a champion you have to be accountable to yourself.

How can you tell someone what to expect of themselves if you cannot inform the same person what to expect from you that day?

Organization is a behavior pattern. Organization is not some concept used to describe what you did. Within the Conscientious Domain of the HEXACO PR Test the Organization scale assesses a tendency to seek order, particularly in one's physical surroundings. The low scorers tend to be sloppy and haphazard; whereas high scorers keep things tidy and prefer a structured approach to tasks.

I have always been a systematic person who appreciates "structure". I did not need to embed this in my behavior. I always possessed a desire to be organized. When I wake up in the morning, I must make my bed. I must organize my night stand in certain way. I always measure the spacing on the edges of my items. I do not hold any third party standard for what I interpret as "neat" or "clean".

I like things being put in their place. Many people make the argument that behavior patterns can be learned, adjusted, and influenced. I think there is truth to that; however, most people will always rebel to their true nature.

A person who hates making the bed is disorganized by nature. There are things the person can do to control their disorganized nature; however, I do not think anyone who doesn't have a burning desire being organized can be great.

That's just my opinion.

Maybe it's possible to rewire your brain to ignite that burning desire. I rewired my capillary veins to go from my kidney to my heart through sheer willpower. On that pretense alone I would say it is possible to rewire your brain to be organized. I would not say it is a highly probable thing to do.

Pure physical trauma changed my body.

I pushed my body to the point of failure and created situations that others before me had literally died from.

Are you that determined to gain a trait?

Most people will pass on that.

On my computer screen I organize a single screen into measured blocks so I can see each item at once. I will adjust the wallpaper to see several things that all go in one spot. I do these adjustments so depending on what I need to see I can see it instantly (at any moment). In my lower left-hand corner will be my email box, the lower right will usually consist of a file search browser, the upper left will consist of the internet browser, and the upper right is usually multiple document bars I scale to full screen when I require it.

This organization saves me time having to open and close things repeatedly to access them. I can efficiently view multiple things at one time without wasting time. If I do not want distraction of background notifications, I "maximize" the one item that requires my focus.

This is an example of how "Organization" breeds "Efficiency".

If you are not doing something effectively, you will fail. Most people will do things ineffective. Imagine there is race and someone wants to race you. There are no rules how you can run. You can run anyway you want. The person you are racing is fast. During the race the person who challenges you decides to sprint two steps left one step right to get to the finish line. Does it matter if your challenger is faster than you? I think you can beat the person that is twice as fast as you by running in a straight line.

The reasons for ineffectiveness can stem from things as simple as "I learned it this way" to "This is the way they taught me." My favorite one is "That's the correct way to do it." Who said you had to do something the way another person said to?

What rule says you cannot change the norm of everything? If you don't plan on maliciously hurting others by your actions, what does it matter?

People who excel to greatness find the most effective way to accomplish their task given their set of circumstances. Great people adapt in a systematic way according to mutual benefit.

The systematic way great people find path to change is by organizing their behavior patterns. Organizing your behavior patterns so your natural character traits shine can help you be great. Being great consists of multiple characteristics.

An Organized person can still lack Diligence.

What is Diligence?

I say it is nearly impossible to expect most people to become something outside their nature. Few can do it. Few can push their body to the point where their body changes. Many psychologists say the human mind learns by "extreme trauma" as an adult. I think this is the way people learn as children too. I am always learning something. I always learn something because I embrace extreme trauma.

I was not always this way.

I will share a story with you.

When I was 10 years old, I did what most children did. I loved playing with toys, using my imagination, reading Goosebumps books, and was obsessed with drawing. I would literally take an entire Saturday to draw. I would make these huge poster boards. I would draw maps of imaginary worlds. I would create continents, name cities, create landmarks, and even design dungeons (a concept I pulled from my favorite video games).

I loved designing imaginary weapons. These were weapons found at each of my landmarks. Swords, axes, spears, you name it. I would draw it. I enjoyed playing video games to make my characters strong. I always wanted to overpower my competition. I never liked "struggling" on a last level or hard boss.

I loved role-playing games for this reason.

I could patiently sit for 8 hours and do a repetitive task (such as fighting a monster over and over) to gradually strengthen my character. I could patiently draw the manifestations of my games for hours as well (the poster boards). Once I became strong enough to move to the next board, I would go. I learned how be patient with these activities. To think the thing I did, that my parents used to complain about all the time, taught me to learn what every parent wants their child to learn:

1. Dedication
2. Patience
3. Planning
4. Attention to Detail.

These are all attributes the military teaches. This is the reason I love the military so much. The organization embodies attributes that came to me naturally.

You know what video games did not teach me?

Resilience.

Tolerance.

Struggle.

So when I was 10 years old I came home from school one day. My brother confronted me about how weak I was. I took a punch in the stomach from my baby sister and folded. I didn't think that was fair. My brother pinned me down to take it. I was caught off guard. My brother wasn't cruel though. He did it as a punishment for being mean to my baby sister and pushing her. In my mind anyone punched in the stomach would say it hurt if they were forced to take a straight shot without warning. I shot back, "I'm not weak". Then one of my other older brothers entered the living room of our apartment. He walked over and joined in the heckling. I was becoming upset. Then one of my brothers suggested something simple.

"If you're so strong why don't you get down and do 10 push-ups."

This seemed simple enough. This was an easy way to prove them wrong. So I went to the kitchen and put myself in the prone position. I told them I could do pushups. Ironically I had never done a push up before. Before this moment I had actually never went down to the floor to do a push-up. I didn't think this was a hard feat. How hard could it be?

I went down and tried to push myself up.

I descended with all the confidence in the world.

When I went down to the ground, I positioned my arms at perfect 90-degree angles.

I pushed.

What happened shocked me.

My arms remained in a locked stance. I pushed as hard as I could.

Nothing.

My arms were stuck.

Soon my arms began to tremble, sweat beaded on my forehead, & fire began to coarse through my stomach. The burning rumble of a firestorm spread throughout out my chest to my arms. My world began to shake.

I fell.

I hit the floor.

Pushups done?

Zero.

In my weakness I had to use my knees to arch myself up. When I looked up to the sky what do you think I saw? Do you think I saw my brothers laughing? Do you think I saw my brothers pointing? Do you think I saw my brothers projecting insults at me?

No.

I saw two faces in utter disbelief.

No one said a word to me.

My brothers were so shocked that I could not do a pushup neither one said anything to me. One of my brothers just looked at me and walked away. The other shook his head and made a sound like blowing out of his mouth.

Kind of like a "Tssh" sound.

I was so humiliated. My brothers could not even find it in them to respond.

My brothers couldn't even laugh or call me a name.

No words needed to be put into their mouths to see what I saw in their faces.

Disappointment.

Weakness.

Disgrace.

Shame.

This moment is an example of "Extreme Trauma". I had a choice at this very young age. I could endure the humiliation and use it to tear down myself. Many people do this. I decided to do something else. The something else was the fire that burned in my stomach from before. I made a vow to myself.

"I will never be this weak again."

I never have. This was my birth of "Diligence".

For the next four weeks I practiced. I practiced doing what they called at the time "Girl Pushups" (Sorry ladies I know it sounds sexist it's just what they called it back then). This is where you have your knees on the ground and do pushups because you are too weak to do a full pushup. After I arrived at a healthy 20 Girl Pushups, I graduated to doing a miniature pushup. The miniature pushup was more of an up and under tester than a pushup. I wish I could describe the pathetic attempt I did but I can't. All you need to know is the exercise had maybe 20% of an actual push up motion. The exercise put all the pressure on my triceps and shoulders. What that half way push up did for me was important. This is something you need to learn as well.

My halfway pushup let me get stronger at a rate I could handle.

Don't make your first dead lift attempt a 600lb lift. You will get injured.

After another two weeks I began doing five full pushups. From then on I made a habit to do pushups with sit-ups. I decided I did not like being called a "Pillsbury Dough Boy" anymore. I could only do 10 sit-ups at the time.

I did pushups every night with my sit-ups.

After 3 months (or 90 days) I was doing 25 pushups and 25 sit-ups.

I would go on to add 5 each a week until I reached 100.

I did this every day of my life until I was 14 years old and could lift weights. Once I went over 100 it became difficult to add 5 pushups a week. So I leveled out by simply doing timed pushups for 2 minutes straight. I would average around 120 – 138. I began to lift weights when I sought a more difficult challenge. I have lifted every day since I was 14 years old (less injuries or proper resting cycles).

Do you think I showed my brothers my new feats? Did you think I ran to them and decided to "Strut like a Peacock"?

The answer is, "I never did."

I did this for myself. I never wanted them to give me the look they gave me in their eyes again. What I sought to do was "prove" them wrong with my "actions". I did not need their affirmation. I was strong. What I needed was for those looks to never come out of their eyes again.

I have never stopped exercising since that day when I was 10 years old. When people ask me what is my goal in the gym? I tell them, "My goal is to be strong." I do not care about the aesthetic part of it.

I am obsessed with being the "strongest".

I am obsessed with being the "hardest" worker in the room.

I am obsessed with being able to "stand" up for myself in any situation.

I am obsessed with being "brave".

The Diligence scale in the Conscientious field assesses a tendency to work hard. Low scorers have little self-discipline and are not strongly motivated to achieve, whereas high scorers have a strong "work ethic" and are willing to exert themselves.

The Conscientious Scale is simple. To work hard, exert yourself, and to push through pain you have to have an extreme trauma in your life.

Mine occurred at a young age. If you are not diligent in your efforts to the point where you will literally die before you give in – you cannot rise to the point of 1%. To be in the 1% you must be the apex of everything. Being the apex means you must be prepared to forfeit everything. If you are not willing to die before you quit, then you lack the necessary diligence to be at the apex. You must go through trauma to attain this level of diligence.

Life throws trauma at you.

You will suffer verbal abuse. You will suffer financial ruin. You will suffer negative comments. You will suffer complete abandonment.

This is trauma. Use trauma to internalize your feelings and push through your trauma. This is the only way you can obtain a high degree of Diligence.

Stop telling yourself, "It was meant to happen. So I'll stop."

That is a quitter talking. Quitters are weak. Quitters make excuses. Quitters say they have no control over their lives and get depressed.

We don't have control over our lives.

Control you attitude. Your attitude is the only thing you can control when it all hits the fan. Your attitude is in your mind. No one tells you how you can or cannot think.

You do.

Now think how to harness your failure into the fuel or components needed to succeed.

This is true Diligence.

Being Diligent will create a drive for being perfect. A person can push through an avalanche if the person already clawed their way through snow. The drive to be perfect, even if you fall short, is the next characteristic of being great.

Perfectionism

I will have it exactly this way.

I will be better than everyone else.

I will be the best because I earn the right.

I will create something that no one else has seen.

I will be perfect because I walk the path no one else will take.

Striving for *Flawed Perfectionism* is an unrealistic goal created in the mind of a person who cannot be satisfied with any standard. There is a state of delusion that almost always sinks in with those that have this trait. *Flawed Perfectionism* can lead to Egoism which can inhibit a person's vision. When a person is not open to criticism and does not hear reason there is an opportunity for failure.

I want to be very careful on this point.

People will be negative and critique you because of they do not believe in you. People will say what you are doing is impossible. People will turn their backs on you. People will refuse to support you due to the statistical abnormality you will come to represent. As a Titan remember people do not like being viewed as small. People who are not Titans do not understand what it is to be one.

Do not take advice about money from someone who is broke.

Similar, do not take advice from someone on marriage who has no successful marriage to illustrate.

These people are the wrong advisers. I am not being condescending by stating these people are not good advisers. Don't call Floyd Mayweather a worse boxer than you when you haven't even won a professional fight.

There is the bottom 10 percentile and there is the top 99 percentile. There are losers and there are winners. The romantic philosophy of "everyone is a winner" is false.

I understand Diligence, Organization, and my undying drive to have Perfectionism. I also know how to be Prudent. This makes me on the higher end of the percentile.

In the frame of Conscientiousness, the Perfectionism scale assesses a tendency to be thorough and concerned with details. Low scorers tolerate some errors in their work and tend to neglect details, whereas high scorers check carefully for mistakes and potential improvements.

Do you remember what I learned in playing video games?

Attention to Detail.

Paying attention to detail is how I could self-teach myself to draw. When others see a straight line, I noticed that there were very subtle angles, curves, and impressions. I noticed in a straight line imperfections create depth. You determine the depth of a shadow in a two-dimensional space through the amount of pressure you put on your pencil. I noticed in order to create realistic faces it required certain "light" strokes in specific directions. Most people do not notice these "light" strokes. This <u>attention to detail</u> allowed me to draft legal contracts 75% accurate despite not being an attorney. This <u>attention to detail</u> translated to reducing my attorney costs on average 30-40% on routine contract work. While I could not entirely draft a legal contract by myself – I could draft it *almost* entirely by myself.

Having someone "fix" something instead of "drafting it from scratch" is a huge cost saver.

Attention to Detail.

I reinforced this concept when I joined the military. When I studied martial arts in Satellite Beach Florida I further reinforced this concept. I studied under a Kendo instructor from Okinawa Japan named Sensei Yamaguchi.

My sensei told me on a number of occasions that my sensei could know everything he needed to know about a person by sparring with them. He explained to me that all the subtleness of people's involuntary movements reveal their true nature. If a person drags their feet, they are lazy. If a person slouches in a chair constantly, they are not inclined to be attentive. If a person will not look you into the eye when discussing a serious subject they are uncomfortable. If a person is gripping their hands too tight, they are tense. When a person doesn't raise their toes before the person steps they are cautious. If a person falls forward walking they are in a rush. You see behavior patterns reveal a lot if you care to pay attention. People are not 100% predictable by observation. People are 95% predictable when they do not know anyone is paying attention. If you are with a person for 8 hours straight their true nature will show. This is why I am always big on meeting people in person.

During my meetings I always acted nonchalant. I acted as if I were not looking at the person I was interested in when they <u>were not</u> talking. I always assumed non aggressive positions. I positioned myself in a non threatening manner. This pre-disposition allowed me to see if people would try to take advantage of me, bully me, or take a get over position on me.

I enjoy appearing weak to unsuspecting people. It allows me to shock them and catch them off guard due to their lack of preparation, assumptions, or when they have a false sense of confidence. A false send of confidence can embolden erroneous actions.

Erroneous actions can be a simple mistake. The mistake can be about a fact the person stated as false but thought I didn't catch on to it. If I know the statement is false and the person is aggressive on a point to simply get their way – I will offer misleading appearances of concern. When the person thinks their error doesn't matter (because he or she thinks they are smarter than me) the person will usually proceed to go on a tangent about a wrong point. I can then choose my time to embarrass them by making a logical observation. The logical observation is always based on what the person said (not me). The fact the person was so quick to jump to conclusions and openly contradict themselves can shake confidence. It is very difficult to argue with your own words. The ability to defend a wrong point is severely impaired if the person's pursuits require other members to base their actions on faulty logic. This is how I catch people off guard. I will inspire dissension in parties who are being unjustifiably aggressive towards me. You can utilize the same tactics.

It is similar to the Kenjitsu stand of Ge-dan. Ge-dan is known as the earth stance. The Ge-dan position has the sword angled towards the ground. The angle of the sword is in a manner where the sharp side is facing the ground.

If you don't understand martial arts and were to see me pointing the cutting side of the blade down (without it put in a position to strike) you may mistake me for vulnerable. If I am looking somewhere else, you may think it is the opportunity to strike. I can parry any move you make from the Ge-dan position. My eyes are looking somewhere else because I know there are two foes. I am observing the unlearned person with my "peripheral vision". With one rotation of the wrist I can cut you across your stomach.

Not very pretty.

That is how I conduct business meetings.

People who do not have Perfectionism as a trait miss what I am doing. I *never* hold my position in a manner where I will "*attack*" you. I do not tolerate aggression for no particular reason. If a person has Perfectionism in them, they will recognize I am not in an aggressive stance. The person will not misjudge my stance for unprepared.

Attention to Detail.

The quality of Perfectionism can be trained. I think Perfectionism is a trait that is more of a skill than a quality. Like any skill Perfectionism can be built by doing things that require you to "pay attention". Mind games on the computer that make you notice number patterns, odd shapes in groups of non similar shapes, and things like this make you pay attention.

Attention to Detail.

Prudence the Great Misidentified Skill

Prudence is often mistaken for being "conservative". Being "conservative" means that fear rules you. A precursor to Prudence is caution. Being cautious does not mean you are struck with fear. Cautious people are not "conservative" or "moderate". Being cautious is a characteristic of prudence.

Being prudent means you have a cautious nature to decide how to best do something "dangerous".

When you are prudent you will never decline a "dangerous" task because of the level of "danger".

When you are prudent it means you will abandon "foolish" tasks no matter the level of "danger".

Being prudent allows you to discover the most cautious way to approach a situation. A prudent person will determine the odds of their success in a given situation. Once the prudent person has discovered the odds, the prudent person will try to play the odds. The prudent person plays the odds when the odds are best in their favor.

Timing & positioning.

That's it.

The Prudence scale assesses a tendency to deliberate carefully and to inhibit impulses. Low scorers act on impulse and tend not to consider consequences, whereas high scorers consider their options carefully and tend to be cautious and self-controlled.

Self Control is required for a person to have Prudence.

Self Control is another pre-cursor to Prudence. There is a beauty about Self Control. Self Control is a skill not a characteristic. You can build Self Control by doing things. Intermittent fasting, meditating, waking up at 4am in the morning (even though you are tired), or getting one more repetition when you are about to give out (make sure you have a spotter) under a squat rack are examples of building Self Control.

A person who lacks Self Control will always allow their mind to quit before their body does.

Self Control and discipline go hand in hand. Discipline is another skill. Prudence is a composition of being: Cautious, Disciplined and having Self Control.

If all three characteristics are skills, not inherited traits, what is Prudence? Prudence <u>can be learned and practiced</u>.

Hone your Prudence by denying bodily desires. Hone Prudence by refusing to sleep with someone on the first night. Hone Prudence by denying your body the food it wants for 14.5 hours (7pm – 930am the next day). Hone Prudence by denying your body the desire to sleep until 10am on Saturday. After you have 6 hours of sleep at 4am wake up.

Prudence uses willpower. You should struggle through tasks to develop your willpower. Willpower will create the foundation for Prudence It requires Willpower to not be impulsive. Impulsive people are not prudent people.

You will notice all the impulse desires I described above might be bad things. Sleeping someone you do not know could cause a disease (or child you do not want), eating whenever you want can lead to excessive weight gain, and sleeping in on Saturday for 12 hours is not considered healthy for an adult.

I think spending 50% of your day "asleep" is a waste of time. Counting 1,456 more hours every year is better. 50 years of this hourly count tallies up to 72,800 more hours to experience life. This amounts to 3,033 more days or 8.3 years. During this "awake" time you're able to: say I love you more, smile with my family more, work extra to provide better for my family, build a better legacy to pass on to my children, or be more successful at being a **Professional Hustler.**

Titans don't avoid life for 8.3 years.

Titans use every moment of their lives to reach for greatness.

As a Titan I cannot afford to waste 8.3 years of my life in a bed doing nothing productive. Next time you feel like sleeping past 6 hours ask yourself,

"Do I want to look back on my life and say that spending 8.3 years in a bed was the most Prudent way to spend my life?"

I think you already know the answer.

Titan or Human?

You decide.

I Made It

I THOUGHT MY career as a **Professional Hustler** was training to become a **Businessman**. Making it to me was having a lasting "business".

In 2015 I began working towards the cause of making a "business". My journey to create a "business" would start on familiar ground. I wanted to work towards something that would benefit my family.

I figured every decision I previously made was preparation for business. I thought my career doing "deals" was for my final great endeavor. I assumed this final great endeavor was to create an enduring "business".

I would go on to discover a different outcome.

During this time I discovered a secret. My parents had kept a secret quiet in my family. Doctors diagnosed one of my sisters with Multiple Sclerosis. My sister began having seizures, blackout spells, and taking medications. These medications were causing very wild mood swings also. Multiple sclerosis (MS) is an unpredictable, often disabling disease of the central nervous system that disrupts the flow of information within the brain, and between the brain and body.

I knew two people in my life affected by MS. Both of them died before the age of fifty. One died almost immediately after forty. The cause of death was officially suffocation while experiencing an epileptic seizure.

My sister affected by MS was born in 1990.

I learned about this disease when my sister was twenty-five years old.

One of the two people who died had passed away the year before. She was a very beautiful person. This was a person held a light that deserved to continue to shine in this world.

Her name was Deidra.

You will notice she is the only person I have named thus far in this book. That is because her name deserves to be remembered by people. Deidra was a woman who refused to let her illness determine her fate. She worked every day of her life until her illness took her.

Deidra was the example of true grit. Deidra had determination and refusal to let anything / anyone tell her she could not become someone. She may have not been a Professional Entrepreneur but she was someone who found a way to support herself financially despite her physical limitations. In some ways that is more than a Professional Entrepreneur can be.

I hope one day to see her again.

The death of this person reminded me how the life of my sister could possibly turn out.

I was very emotional during this time. My sister described her experience at her last doctor's visit when I found out about her diagnosis. The physician explained she would eventually lose her motor skills, not conduct basic activities and become helpless. She was very shaken by the prognosis. Another fact equally devastated my sister. The physician informed my sister there was no known cure. I was emotional. I was emotional because both individuals I knew that had MS died before 50. One died around 48 and the other at 42.

Was I looking at a beautiful young girl that would die in 17 years?

I could not accept that.

There had to be something I could do. I had no idea how I would discover this option. I thought about what I could do with the skill set I had.

I was a **Professional Hustler.**

Around the same time I was being pestered by a former pack member of mine. My former pack member wanted me to come to Jacksonville, Florida. This was not something I was in the mood for. The pack member was insistent on me coming to his house. My former pack member told me I had to meet a special person. I needed to work on a project the following month with him. If I ignored him I knew that this could sour a potential deal we had been contemplating. As a **Professional Hustler** a substantial amount of value is found in developing interpersonal relationships. The lack of development in an interpersonal relationship can create a void in your pack.

I always "ate" what I "killed".

Failing to pay attention to this potential gripe could have meant a member of the "pack" would stray.

Therefore, I had to answer the phone. I watched the phone ring two, three, four more times. After many calls and persistence I answered the phone.

"Chris I have been trying to get a hold of you all mourning."

I spoke to my former pack member for a few minutes. After hearing my former pack member out, I acquiesced to the desires of my former pack member. I made a drive to Jacksonville.

During my drive I prayed. I prayed that somehow, someway God would show me a way to hone my skills to find a treatment for my sister. I also cried.

If you meet me you understand I am not a crier.

I maybe shed tears once every year or so. If I do cry it is usually for something sentimental about my daughter. I love my daughter with all my heart. My daughter is very precious to me. I treat my daughter like she is precious to me. For someone that does not require emotional pacification I can be very affectionate to someone I love. I have a baby sister who lives in California who has a similar effect on me. She is my sister. We share the same father but have different biological mothers. The other person that passed away was someone who remarried her mother. She is a second mother to me. I also call her mother "Mima" which means "My Mom". My Mima's husband was a good man. His name was Wes. He served in the military. He labored through an entire military career with MS. Imagine that. This man did road marches and would faint rather than back out. Talk about determination. He died a few years after retiring. My respect is immense for his determination to serve his country his entire "healthy" life. Wes could have been medically discharged. Wes never accepted that. Remember attributes of perseverance like that if you want to be successful.

You will need to persevere against all odds if you want to be successful in the career path of a **Professional Hustler**.

Before I had my daughter I would say I cried once every 2 or 3 years. Girls have a way of changing a man. Hopefully, the change is for the better. I have a habit of giving preferential treatment to women. The women in my life have unlocked my heart to be compassionate towards those not recognized often. As a result, I have a tendency to look at women as people. Seems like a normal thing right? That was an odd thing in the past. The #metoo movement is bringing balance to the way women are treated. Some men will unfortunately get dragged into the publicity of it all; however, the majority deserves what is coming to them.

The #metoo movement does have downside.

I think many women (not all) are so focused on trying to get the same rights as men they don't take time to study men. Men haven't had to study women for a long time. Women traditionally fit a gender role. Now they are redefining their roles. So men are also upset at having to put effort towards women. There are two sexes on this planet. We both run businesses. So it is important for both to learn each other.

Independent means alone.

I don't intend to say women are destined to be alone.

I don't intend to say men are destined to be alone.

I mean independent means literally alone…like with no one.

I think a strong independent man is just as bad as a strong independent woman. Anytime someone only develops independence skills (i.e. independent) they cannot work in a team.

This is destructive on several levels and has nothing to do with equal rights.

Personally, I like traditional roles where one person worries about the well-being of the family's legacy (i.e. children) and the other worries about providing for the family.

Increasingly, we see a diverge from this path in today's modern society. As a result it is harder to find a good team player in this structure.

I've heard people say, "Men treat their women like their mothers." I wrote her birthday love letters every birthday until I left her home. I still write my mother love letters. We should cherish mothers. Real men understand this and protect their mothers.

Protection is an ingrained characteristic in **Professional Hustlers** who lead Red Teams. **Professional Hustlers** also recognize independence cannot get in the way of team cohesiveness.

Professional Hustlers do not believe being alone (independent) is the best way to do things.

Professional Hustlers survive (get by) alone (independently) but do not thrive (earn comfortably) alone.

Remember the wolf pack leader?

Now you understand why I trail behind my troop.

So I was off to Jacksonville, Florida to meet the person who would end up being the Chief Executive Officer (CEO) of a biotechnology company I would incorporate. Little would I understand how important this event would come to be in my future.

As I arrived, I walked into the house of a former super bowl champion. My former pack member was a two-time champion of the Philadelphia Eagles and San Francisco 49ers. My former pack member won his super bowls back in the late 1970's and early 1980's. He wore two super bowl championship rings. I have a good way of connecting with the best. Champions are Titans or members of the Greek god family. My former pack member would go on to sit on our board for about a year. My former pack member would have to resign to take personal time due to a family illness. Once I entered my former pack member's house, they greeted me. My former pack member sat me at his dining room table. I saw someone close to my age. The man was in his later 30's and sat at the table on a laptop computer.

My former pack member sat me down and said, "Chris I asked you to come up here because I needed you to meet someone very important. You all are about the same age. So I thought you both should get together. He has some amazing stuff you have to see."

I did not understand what this man was talking about.

We will call the man at the table Dr. C.

Dr. C was an astute, intelligent man who had a familiar predisposition to me. I recognize people who come from humble beginnings to make something of their lives. When I looked at this man he was confident, well spoken, but had an accent that made me feel like he was one of my friends from high school.

Still, I didn't care.

I wanted to leave.

Despite feeling a desire to leave I sat down at the table and said, "No problem. I'm happy to look at what you need me to see. Since it is important."

I didn't act condescending, annoyed, or impatient. A characteristic important in a **Professional Hustler** is having Prudence. Remember Self Control? I contained my emotions and kept my composure to listen to Dr. C's presentation. Dr. C showed me slides about different molecular compositions of peptides. The presentation focused mainly on desalination and water cleaning. My former client had a waste treatment and removal company for contaminated water. What I saw was a giant presentation on me raising money for my former client. I had a good reputation for raising money.

Great.

This important meeting was for him to push his own agenda.

I was nearly checked out until I saw something interesting.

Dr. C showed me a small section entitled "Human Applications". In this section Dr. C showed me a lot of amazing things. One video struck a chord with me. The section that struck a chord with me was a video of lab mice. The lab mice engineered had no immune system. The lab mice were genetically altered to have Multiple Sclerosis.

I focused on the screen.

Then Dr. C showed me something special. An injection of a special formulated peptide changed the lab mice in a 24-hour period. The lab mice went from dragging their hind legs to full-blown running around their cages.

It floored me.

Here was something that was statistically impossible.

How could I pray to find a meaningful way to apply my skills and within 2 hours discover what I asked for?

I prayed to find a path to help my sister cope with her disease. On this screen I was looking at preclinical research data, with lab mice, that represented promising steps towards an application that could possibly help my sister.

I asked if Dr. C had any experience doing anything successful.

Dr. C had exactly *"one"* reference.

Dr. C informed me he presented a similar peptide derivative he developed with his mentor. This peptide derivative was successful in getting a 5mm USD investment. Because of developing this technology, they gave Dr. C and his mentor a small equity stake. Dr. C was appointed as the Chief Research Officer for the technology. Dr. C was chosen to be involved on a scientific panel for a very well-known pharmaceutical billionaire in California. The pharmaceutical billionaire was the investor. Although this was Dr. C's only reference I was keen enough to use common sense.

I was not a scientist.

I had no way of qualifying what I was seeing.

I used common sense association to determine the credibility of what I was seeing.

"If a well known pharmaceutical billionaire believed in the last thing this man helped develop…Dr. C must be showing me something tangible."

This was an example of a "Middle Space".

The man had done "one" deal. Dr. C did not have a long list of references. Dr. C's one reference would blow out most people. To another seasoned person all Dr. C would have possessed was a record of "one deal" that might fail.

I did not see Dr. C's accomplishment this way.

This man provided his first scientific application for commercialization to a man who built his fortune on judging promising opportunities.

I thought, "Dr. C must have a mind that can produce something."

I have too many stories like this that convince me of God's existence. I am not a traditional religious person. I am very logical. The logic of probability has led me to believe there is no such this as randomness.

Here are basic math concepts. Probability measures the likelihood of an event occurring. Expressed mathematically, probability equals the number of ways a specified event can occur, divided by the total number of all possible event occurrences. For example, if you have a bag containing three marbles -- one blue marble and two green marbles -- the probability of grabbing a blue marble sight unseen is 1/3. There is one possible outcome where the blue marble is selected, but three total possible trial outcomes -- blue, green, and green. Using the same math the probability of grabbing a green marble is 2/3.

In the Law of Probability there is something called Zero-Probability Events. These Zero-Probability Events do not mean that the events will not happen; however they eliminate the chance of randomness because certain variables can be set to create a situation where every outcome is in fact a Zero-Probability Event.

Sound complicated?

I can be that way.

Putting it simple – I use the law of Probability to justify things happen for a reason. I have a paradoxical statement that guides my convictions

"I believe in the predestination of freewill."

I will let you chew on that for a while.

It was at the moment I heard Dr. C's reference I decided there was enough substance to base my decision.

I would believe in Dr. C.

I stared at the screen. After my decision to believe in Dr. C I arrived at another conclusion. I believed I found the purpose of my career. I was built to this point to identify the "opportunity" with Dr. C to help save my sister.

Anyone who knows me knew I only did this for my family.

I would be the person to capitalize him for the benefit of my family in a "business".

I shared the story about my sister with Dr. C. Dr. C didn't show too much emotion as he responded to me. Dr. C then said, "Well if we get the money we need, maybe we can help your sister one day."

I leaned over in my chair and made the following statement, "I have no idea how I will do this but I will fund your project."

I would labor for a full year understanding advanced biology.

Dr C was the one person on the scientific team that had the patience to teach me what I needed to know about the field to properly raise capital.

I told Dr. C to be patient with me and he was. I appreciated that aspect of Dr. C. At least Dr. C was patient in the process to raise money. Many people lack this patience. The lack of patience is why startups go nowhere.

Quick up front lesson on startups.

<u>Never raise money for someone who will not put a substantial sum of their own money into something.</u> **The person who does not put substantial money into a startup will never value your efforts. The person who does not put substantial money into a startup will act recklessly with other people's money.**

Remember that lesson.

After one year of learning biology, I could translate how companies who statistically run in the red their entire career are fundamentally sound investments. In biotechnology there is a premium paid for the likelihood of a particular application entering the market. **The premium is up front cash to you the research company.** The big pharmaceutical companies abandoned research and development about 25 years ago. The big pharmaceutical companies did this to make sure they did not waste money on bad technology. Smaller companies would weed out technology that did not show promise of being admitted to basic clinical trials. Due to the departure of a leading authority (remember I talked about *Disorganization*) anyone could raise money based on pre-clinical data. The pitch of a new company was then based on the "likelihood" an application would be admitted to clinical trials. If a biotech company's technology makes it to clinical trials the startup is typically given a deal. This deal comes from one of the "big players" in the pharmaceutical space (Purdue, Merck, Johnson & Johnson). If the application successfully passes an initial phase I, the research company typically realizes a cash out event. This is called a milestone payment. The milestone payment increases with each successful phase and the terms are better. The more a person can capital raise in a pre-clinical setting (to get further along) the more value the upfront cash payment will be. A person can make millions of dollars on a failed clinical application if the research shows promise.

If a technology fails clinical trials, it does not mean the research was not valuable. Often failed clinical trials serve as basis for successful future treatments.

When a milestone is given, the big pharmaceutical company typically agrees to fund the remainder of the research. It is at this point a big company will merge the company into its ownership. Typically, a small research company's founders are left some form of royalty or small equity stake. Big companies take the risk of exploring a new application. Only 1 out of 10 new drugs will make it to market. The one that makes it usually recovers the losses from the others. The one that makes it through all clinical trials is wildly profitable. Just think about how long chemotherapy has been going (it's into the trillions now). It is an odds game. The big pharmaceutical companies play the odds.

Not so different from a **Professional Entrepreneur or Hustler** is it?

After I figured out how biotechnology companies work, how the research is valued, and how/why larger pharmaceutical companies buy research I raised a substantial amount of money.

I had to put my entire reputation on the line to make this one work. I had to create separate successful ventures to instill confidence in this "wild" and "ambitious" idea. The structure I proposed had never previously been done. I had to create and inspire a sense of confidence in nothing tangible (no assets, no intellectual property, and no founder cash at stake). I had to do all this while retaining the majority of control and equity in the company.

Remember Dr. C's last 5 million deal? Dr. C gave away 100% of the intellectual property and 80% of the stock. **Yeah those bad terms are the deals available in the pre-clinical biotechnology space.** If I wanted to build a "business" to help my sister we had to retain control. Up until this point I had a decent track record (if you remember from earlier) on "deals". I was 6-5-1 at this point (not counting any deals past 2015). I knew I had to approach people who valued my track record. I had to focus on perceived "value" versus "equity" or "cash flow". I had to focus on non industry professionals.

On this one I had to be the *Hustler*.

I had to make people believe in someone with: no track record in business, one commercial product to his name, still held a job somewhere else (not his full-time thing), no credible company (not formed yet), a mentor who could create commercially viable technologies that wasn't all the way committed and the only verifiable facts on Dr. C were grant funding on unrelated experiments. The cherry on top was it was because of his university level position (his main job).

To make you understand how hard this was – it is considered a Zero Probability Event.

I found no other reference in my research of someone doing what I did. No one I researched had previously accomplished my proposal. I do not say this as a way to boast. I say this to give you an example of how pure willpower and passion can make you succeed. No biotechnology I researched had ever raised in excess of 1mm USD cash on no intellectual property ownership. More importantly, no biotechnology I researched ever raised this much money and through the process only relinquished about 4% of its equity. No documented biotechnology company I researched had ever received an underwriting agreement for in excess of 50mm with a "waiver" of the upfront fee charge.

This is called a "Statistical Abnormally".

I would go on to do the following capital raise performance: $1,144,436.27 of working capital from May 2nd 2017 to May 16th 2018, approximately $2,531,792.38 in solvency capital, secure best efforts underwriting commitment from a small offshore US Registered Bank for $100,000,000, and obtain a signed licensing agreement for exploratory research in Vietnam with an upfront payment due to the biotechnology company for a fixed fee of $1,000,000 from a Vietnamese Partner.

I make these statements to inspire you not to boast.

I did this by inspiring people we would go public one day in Bermuda, on the Bermuda Stock Exchange (BSX).

When a person puts their mind to do something it is possible for impossible things to occur. **Zero Probability Events can occur.** No one would believe in a Research Scientist at a small university, who could only afford to put up $5,000 towards his company's incorporation, and only had "one" pending deal. No one would believe that this research scientist would work with a team of people that would go on to win a United States Agriculture Contract Research and Development Agreement (CRADA). They reserve CRADA for the highest research quality available on advance issues that are considered important to National Security. We made this CRADA possible through my family estate's $100,000 investment, my independent reputation as a financial professional, intellectual property from Dr. C's mentor, Dr. C's teaching stint and my capital raising efforts.

With all this I accomplished a Zero Probability Event.

This is no small feat.

This deal was never about money. Remember you attract what you are not what you want. I was a person who devoted myself to the cause of trying to save my sister. My words were real, from the heart and passionate.

I argue I was the most passionate person at the company.

I started this project for one reason and one reason only. I wanted to help contribute to research that could benefit my sister. That was my only motivation. The drive I had to refuse to see my sister waste away fueled my drive. I combined everything I had and played a high stakes game.

If I failed on something that looked speculative I would lose my reputation. If I failed on something that my regulators felt was "unsuitable" for my clients they would pressure me to give up my license. No third party cared about my sister. I cared about my sister.

I had to decide to legally disclose everything about an opportunity, and despite the apparent conflicts of interest agree to pursue a highly probable failure.

I had all the disclosures in place, the conflict letters, and the proper documentation method to show my clients how "their money" would compensate me. I tried to be very meticulous with how I disclosed everything. I would not let some technicality snag me for trying to devote myself full-time to my sister's well being. My close attorney friend authored a phenomenal conflict letter that put any issue to bed. Despite covering the legal basis, I did what most financial advisors avoid. I put my client's money into a startup I had significant influence over. The easy thing would be to decline the opportunity to contribute towards saving my sister and worry about myself. The compliance nightmare this create for my financial advisor firm was very real. Still, I would not shy away from helping my sister.

I put my entire firm's reputation on the line to make this company work. I researched other comparable firms. In my research I realized something very interesting. I realized that biotechnology companies that can complete field trials in agriculture sell for a lot of money. A hidden blessing in this project was that the human application peptides had agriculture applications. One of Dr. C's close research scientist that had mentored him early on was part of our team. We will call this mentor Dr. J. Dr. J was a man that created more scientifically applicable patents than anyone in his field (that I could research). Due to Dr. J's lack of business knowledge every successful deal that Dr. J did… they cheated Dr. J out of. They cheated Dr. J out of every deal except one. This one deal Dr. J still had possessed proven patented technology in a very late stage III field trial. The technology showed so much promise it was picked up by the lead citrus producer in Florida. A New York Times article chronicled its success.

Dr. J should be a multi-millionaire 10x over but he wasn't. I realized the value of the research / deal was not in Dr. C. The value was in Dr. J's willingness to give his promising technology to us. Dr. J trusted Dr. C explicitly. I did what no one else did for Dr. J. I told Dr. C to offer Dr. J more than anyone ever did. I also insisted to Dr. C we do it a "non-contingent" basis. I instructed Dr. C to allocate up front a large part of the company to

Dr. J at incorporation. I did this before Dr. J created anything of value. I was giving Dr. J what no one else had ever cared to give Dr. J.

I was giving conviction to Dr. J that he was enough.

I made sure Dr. C gave Dr. J "security" and "affirmation". This action would mean that we would never steal Dr. J's technology from him like everyone else had done. Dr. J would later watch my capital raising efforts. My performance would make him believe in me. Dr. J would believe in me so much he would give all ownership stakes he had in the company that held the "promising" 8 year track record technology. Our partnership to form this new biotechnology company centered on Dr. C managing Dr. J's expectations and me performing all of the financial related items. Dr. J would be the only person to show me genuine appreciation for my efforts.

Dr. J created me a custom crystal etched model of our peptide in appreciation. It is what I consider my "trophy" for "winning". It lights up with an LED light at the base to illuminate. It sits on my night stand to remind me of my accomplishments.

If you are reading this Dr. J…Thank you.

Thank you, Dr. J for appreciating the sacrifice I gave to make the company what it is today.

Even when the snakes came in to take advantage of my situation (and illegally take a my family estate's shares) you gave me something worth more than the stock.

You gave me acknowledgment you couldn't be where you are without me.

No one else ever thanked me or recognized me.

I will always remember Dr. J for that reason.

I left the shares alone because sometimes money is a curse. The money they make from illicit earnings will bear a sour crop. Sometimes the best way to get someone back is to let them do the bad things they did.

I worked 12 hours a day to make this company happen. Everyone else treated it like a part-time job. I remember getting on the phone with one of our future scientists to explain to their attorney why we were giving them ownership. Funny, I had to explain to an attorney why someone who paid $0 for their stock should accept it. That one always makes me a laugh when I think about it. As time passed, I began to exclusively work on the company. During this time I saw myself as a **Businessman**. I rationalized that if I could incorporate this company, completely build the entire corporate infrastructure, raise 100% of the money, and identify how to utilize Dr. J's research I deserved to hold the title of **Businessman.**

I was no longer a **Professional Hustler** I concluded.

I was a unique **Businessman.** I found myself a top-level executive position by exploiting an opportunity in an *Emerging Concept.* The *Emerging Concept* came from the United States agriculture market's *Disorganization.* For *Personal Reasons* Dr. J gave us an entire intellectual property portfolio. I had all three reasons combined into one deal. More importantly, the biotechnology deal centered on helping my sister. Could you blame me for thinking this one was my divine purpose?

Along the way I structured the company where most of the ownership would go to Dr. C. A tiny percentage of the company would go to my family estate that my children would benefit from.

When the new CEO found ways to exclude my shares in a reincorporation and rebranding, he did not cheat me. He cheated children.

I chose a vulnerable position on stock because I did not want the problems of being a "control person". I had "conflicts". The rules around Regulation D prevented stockholders from taking more than $50,000 in a capital raise. I could not work for more than a year on a weak salary like that. Store Managers at Wal-mart make more salary compensation than the rules for Regulation D allow. I decided to have "no official ownership". I had to make the hard decision to own nothing in the thing I would build. Who else would give their full-time attention and reputation for $4,250 per month on a highly probable failure?

The answer?

The guy who wanted to save his sister.

Most of our stakeholders wanted to keep doing their own thing while assisting the company. Most could not stop earning money to try a new venture. I was the only one willing to do this "full time".

A close friend ran his own legal practice, Dr. C had a university position, Dr. J taught and held various consulting jobs making "peptides", and our Clinical Officer ran a hospital. My pack member was a retired NFL star.

To Dr. C's credit he did repeatedly ask me if I wanted stock. I turned it down due to conflicts and rules created in a "Saturated Securities Market".

With a Series 65 there were rules that applied to me which did not apply to the common **Businessman.**

I would learn later it does not pay to be a license holder in an unconventional business environment. I should have not refused the stock as well. I should have just closed my practice when this decision was being proposed. I didn't. I thought I could still do both.

I figured my personal compensation would come later in an Initial Public Offering. Dr. C always said he would "take care" of me from his side. Who knows if Dr. C will do what he said. Maybe Dr. C will be the one person who does not require any communication for 5 years and his conscious forces him to do the right thing. Time will tell. Although I was doing the most pivotal parts to create this company's value (i.e. raise money to make all the commercialization possible) I figured it didn't matter.

Dr. C knew what I did. Dr. C was there every step of the way. None of the research meant anything if no one could find the money to commercialize it. So I became what I thought was a close friend and brother to Dr. C.

I trusted Dr. C explicitly and implicitly. Remember, I also was becoming convinced this was a "divine" set up. I became emotionally connected. Emotions can blind you when you are using it to drive you. Emotions can make you "impulsive".

I structured the company where Dr. C was the sole decision maker on everything. I could officially make no real decision (despite my board position) because all the shareholder's proxy votes resided with Dr. C. The majority of the Board would always be carried by Dr. C casting a vote one way or another.

This arrangement made sense to me. I could not control the company but I had the CEO's ear. I felt like I was the Vizier to the Sultan. The Sultan would keep his Vizier close because he depended on him. I mean no one else raised money. So I felt secure in my position.

Plus Dr. C was a PhD research scientist who lectured around the world on prostate cancer. Dr. C had been cited well over 1,000 times, was extremely presentable, well spoken, and from everything I could judge had a good character. I was comfortable at a position of vulnerability if it was with this man.

So I worked under this pretense.

I would "time" my exit and take my personal "compensation" later once a qualified attorney determined it legally allowed.

I created one milestone after another with the support of the scientific research team. The team produced results that no common sense person could understand. I had the task of explaining this in simple 3rd grade words.

My approach worked.

I performed. I raised the money needed to culminate into an open line of communication with the United States Department of Agriculture. We worked for 6 months back and forth negotiating the terms of the agreement. I led the negotiations to merge Dr. J's membership interest in an 8 year agriculture field trial solving a pressing issue in Citrus. We acquired the membership interest in the company that the New York Times detailed. Dr. J's technology beat out every other scientist. I asked my brother to originate an underwriter for our company for me to negotiate with. The underwriter committed to us because my brother organized the meeting in Singapore. I pulled in my close friend as an attorney to oversee the entire company's legal issues. I gave my close friend a flat $50,000 legal fee out of my own pocket. I also negotiated some stock for his personal compensation. We brought on a person I will call Hustler J. Hustler J was to originate the international investor base for the underwriter. Hustler J came at the referral of my close friend's law firm. We went to Bermuda at the advice of Hustler J. The trip to Bermuda worked. We were able to get a signed Underwriting Agreement to underwrite a convertible debt issue in Bermuda. We were off to the races.

I was the first substantial investor in our company. I paid for my close friend's legal fee of $50,000. I then made my family estate put the first $50,000 into the corporate bank account. I believed in this business. I put in money when no one else put in money.

The CEO of the company, Dr. C, owned over 90% of the shares. Guess what Dr. C put in?

Dr. C put in about $15,000.

Remember my lesson about how much money a start-up owner should put in from earlier? This amount will come to play a big part in future developments of this company.

I put over $100,000 of my personal money and family estate towards the company. This does not count whatever I spent on the company to keep it moving. I venture to say I was close to $200,000. The founding shareholders, except for Dr. C, have no hard dollars invested in the company. Dr. J put his life's work into the company so it is unfair to say Dr. J put in $0; however, Dr. J did not put in any cash. Dr. C's $15,000 was the only actual cash given by founding shareholders outside of my family's estate at incorporation.

A violation of one of the Golden Rules can be found in this narration. Read the Richest Man in Babylon to get a deeper insight into these rules. The decision I made to structure the company this way showcased lack of Prudence on my part. My high emotional connection to this company caused my hasty desire to perform. *I started this for my sister. I did not think about the money.* I was not a trained scientist. So what was I doing in the biotechnology field? I was evolving into a market I was new to. I came into this market because of a desire to protect someone I loved. Although I was new to this field, I would achieve record setting milestones due to my drive to "protect". I would hit these milestones because of the tenacity I had as a **Professional *Hustler***.

Remember, I said this was a win right?

It is and was a win as a **Professional Hustler**.

Do you remember what I thought I was?

I thought I was a **Businessman**.

Let's keep following this story. I want you to see how this story comes together, unfolds, and inevitably concludes. There are a lot of lessons I am trying to teach you in this story.

A major +1mm USD investor I helped organized from California invited us to see him in Marina Del Rey. The investor gave the invitation once we received a written response from the USDA that our agreement would be signed. Dr. C and I went early in anticipation of the CRADA agreement being sent to us. While we were at the Marriot hotel in Marina Del Rey they delivered the contract.

Dr. C and I looked at each other with astonishment of our timing.

Dr. C printed the contract out and I brought out my special Mont Blanc pen.

We signed the highest awarded research contract that the United States Government can award. Imagine that. Here were two people against the odds who accomplished something no one had ever done before. We beat out Monsanto, and all the major agriculture companies to take the lead on solving a huge problem in the USDA. I could not describe the immense amount of joy I felt during this moment.

Here was a business I literally had to do the Bylaws myself, incorporate myself, file myself, and open up its first bank account. Now we had a business that was the recipient of the highest research contract available from a United States Government Agency.

We celebrated but we still needed to get more money.

I called up my legal friend and asked him about Bermuda. He told me he had just the guy to help us with the large-scale raise.

My close friend referred me to a former international banker from Deloitte. This man was the embodiment of my former Forex CEO <u>with one exception</u>. This man had very obvious signs of apparent wealth. My close friend who was an attorney affirmed this man. This former international banker had owned his own broker dealer before the regulatory changes. This former international banker had also called the failure of my former Forex CEO's demise. This former international banker was keen enough to perceive the Prime Broker having liquidity issues. For this reason I have an ironic reference. The man was someone that an executive of a former company should have listened to and this is a man I should have ignored.

How ironic is that?

I would lose despite doing the opposite of what I thought should have been done.

We will call this man Hustler J. Hustler J was a well spoken, internationally privileged person whose family was verifiably wealthy. My misjudgment of these facts would cause my first business mistake. I would blunder through nearly $150,000 at the advice of Hustler J. Upon seeing the issues of my blunder I would attempt to diversify some capital raised into a failed investment. After spending through nearly $150,000 I would cost the company an additional $150,000 trying to recover the losses incurred because of the advice of Hustler J. In total my business decisions would lose our company close to $300,000. I was attempting to make up for my decision to follow Hustler J's advice.

Hustler J's advice was to ignore listing in the United States (as I originally wanted to do) and register an offshore convertible debt offering in

Bermuda without adhering to our underwriting agreement. Hustler J said he could get his family to invest if it was done properly. Hustler J selected the Listing Sponsor, the Auditor, and then the structure. My close friend was new to the entire concept and presented Hustler J for what he was. Hustler J was a third party, former banker who had verifiable facts. Remember what I said about **Hustlers**? **Hustlers** <u>usually have one or two verifiable facts</u>. Hustler J's two facts were: 1) his family was wealthy and 2) he worked for Deloitte. I combined this with "confirmation by association" which was another fatal flaw. I thought because he was "associated" with the law firm that he was "confirmed" by it. I never thought to ask my close friend if he verified any of his investors. I just "assumed" it happened. We will go on to see how that "assumption" turns out.

It would turn out my close friend was learning at the same rate as me. A major fact that convinced me of Hustler J was his family's wealth. Hustler J made me believe his high-net-worth family connections would perform once we listed our security in Bermuda.

Hustler J told me if he designed this structure we would have to work out compensation for Hustler J. Hustler J needed a lot of money upfront. We negotiated it down because our budget wasn't in the six digits range. Hustler J said he needed "big money". They hustled me into believing it because of my misclassification of Hustler J's involvement with my close friend's law practice. Hustler J made me think there was only value to do the deal if we agreed to diversify some of his raised capital into real estate deals. My close friend was a real estate attorney. I knew there would be no issue with any real estate project selected if my close friend signed off on it.

I agreed. Dr. C informed he would follow my lead.

So we paid a sizable 5 figure fee to Hustler J.

Hustler J told me the process would take 90 days, and about $100,000. I would spend the next 15 months & nearly $150,000 trying to complete this "quick 90 day process". I would also work with people who were the most arrogant people I had ever worked with. In addition to severe arrogance I would also find out about two more surprises. I would find out about excessive charges for limited work and the revenge that comes with firing someone on a small island.

Never fire a service provider in a small community. The people you fire will road block you at every turn. Everything is personal on a small island. Everyone knows the other person you are searching for.

I went into one foreign market without the proper legal framework in place to enforce people's contractual commitment when my diversified investment failed. My second foreign market entrance was at the advice of Hustler J who ended up disappearing mid way. Hustler J disappeared because "he wasn't getting paid enough."

Isn't that interesting?

Hustler J had promised millions of dollars from connections he said he knew (we would later come to find out he just called around and never met them). Then Hustler J abandoned a 10mm dollar commission because he wasn't making enough money?

Let's analyze this for a minute.

A man says he knows he has enough investors to invest into a project. The man also says he knows the structure they will invest into. The man shows obvious wealth and embeds himself into an organization to appear trustworthy (a law firm although he is not an attorney). The man recommends this structure under the explanation he knows the market. The man then gets paid up front. The man's payment is to send us to people who charge us more money. The professionals that we are directed to tell us the information we received from the man is incorrect. The man says not to worry about it. The man says once we are complete with the task to let him know so he can pour in the money. The man always affirms his interest in obtaining funds for real estate projects because our payment was "too low". Not to worry, the man always states the commission is high for him. We respected him enough to pay enough money for about 30-days worth of effort. In the backend everything will even out. Then we go over budget by over $50,000. We go over the man's estimated schedule by 9 months. Despite the time, effort and cost spent we complete this task we get to the last stage. There is only one last round of work. We advise the man we are done after all the delays. The man then says he moved out of the city and doesn't know if he can do anything because he hasn't been paid lately.

That is an example of how a *Hustler can burn down your house.*

Never do arrangements like this.

If Hustler J had even 1% of what he said he had – we would have earned some performance from Hustler J. Instead Hustler J literally "left" the city. Who leaves 10mm on the table when it was in the bag less than 7 months ago? I have managed deals for a decent amount of time. Investor money does not evaporate on a 100mm offering – especially when the opportunity could yield as much as the biotechnology company could (verifiably). We were in partnership with the United States Department of Agriculture. How much of a reference do you really need?

I was *hustled* as a **Businessman**.

Maybe I'm too harsh. In Hustler J's defense he did end up originating a few million dollars on a separate real estate deal the following year with my close friend. It was unrelated but it kept the faith up. Maybe this guy could do something despite the issues I experienced. Maybe he can perform for a real estate deal that is straight forward, but he just bit off more than he could chew? Who knows?

After finishing the offering the way Hustler J directed the Underwriter was asking me when the offering would be complete. The offering I took our company down at the behest of Hustler J did not conform with their standards. The international investor confidence Hustler J claimed was <u>nonexistent</u>.

I was in a bind.

I had to make up the amount of money wasted at the advice of Hustler J. I inquired to a relationship of mine who owned a refinery moving commodities in and out of Africa. The risk was high, but the returns were attractive.

As a **Businessman** I did not do the most important part of a high return investment. I failed to make sure I had a skilled "Prudent" **Professional Entrepreneur** involved in the shipment.

The **Professional Entrepreneur** must always be involved in the riskiest part of an aggressive transaction. In the case of this transaction it would be the "physical transport" of the commodity itself.

I thought I was in business now.

So, I did what I thought all businesspeople should do. I allowed the contract to be managed at the direction of an employee from the third-party shipping company responsible for moving it.

My result?

The shipment was stolen.

The money was lost.

I had two strikes against me making decisions in business.

I consulted with my CEO of the biotechnology company. At this point I was thinking "I need to get someone besides me to raise some money". I informed our CEO that we needed someone with the right "pedigree". The CEO, Dr. C, agreed with my points. I had about 1.5mm pending but our company needed a lot more money. Biotechnology companies' burn through 100's of millions of dollars in research costs. We needed to put gas on our human applications. We needed someone with the right background to ask for 100mm USD.

I thought this man would be the future of the company. I brought in a phenomenal performer who I considered very much a mentor. I thought this man was "honorable". How and why I came to that conclusion is another story. The man was a "Rainmaker". The man rang the stock bell at major exchanges, managed as much as 13bn under management and co-created the first publicly traded Index ETF. I spent 60 days trying to convince the "Rainmaker" to pay attention to this company. I also spent significant time asking him to pick up the mess on what Hustler J had created. Once the investment turned south on the gold deal (I had structured as a Promissory Note) I realized that I needed someone much more experienced. More importantly, I needed someone who could make better decisions. It was at this point I started realizing something. Although I could hustle something out of nothing, I could not make something into everything. I needed a "Rainmaker". I needed a man with a public resume that would do the things required to bring this company main stream.

As I write this book, I hope the man will be my good judgment to replace the former leadership. The former leadership would fail me, abandon me, and turn its back on me despite the efforts I gave for the company. Remember I do not walk away with nothing at the end of this.

I am not a fool.

I am a **Professional Hustler** who has "Prudence" in my *"profession"*. I could have been a prudent Businessman if I had the experience to make the "right" decisions. At that time, I lacked experience.

Lacking experience does not make you a failure.

Lacking experience is just that. You lack experience. That's it. Don't get down on yourself. If you played sports your first practice probably sucked. That didn't mean you were a failure. You have to keep practicing.

After getting our Rainmaker signed on, something else began to surface. The Securities & Exchange Commission (SEC) had noticed I invested client money into a company I *appeared* to control. This company was the biotechnology company. The SEC has the right to make sure no abuse is happening. I want to be very clear on this point. There is nothing wrong with a regulator making sure you did not take your client's money and buy yourself a Ferrari. *The issue is that is not what usually happens.* I want you to understand something about regulators. Regulators who have "proactive" stances are usually in "Saturated Markets".

If a Professional Entrepreneur recognizes an opportunity within a Saturated Market, there must be a hard exit date.

Pay close attention to one of my decisions as a **Businessman**. I decided to invest into an "African Gold Transaction to earn double the money." I decided to invest company resources into an unrelated item to make up the company losses I suffered because of Hustler J. I also took a small portion of raised money from my previous clients to conduct this activity.

Despite my desire to make the company successful it might appear an African gold deal could be sketchy way to use biotech monies.

Dealing gold out of Africa is usually tied to some scam or Ponzi scheme in our mainstream media. To a person who is uneducated, inexperienced, or lacks the knowledge of how international transactions work this is the biggest red flag imaginable if the investment does not work.

On the voluntary disclosure of my financial advisor documents to the Securities & Exchange Commission I pulled a group of investigators from the Securities & Exchange Commission whose organization just finished investigations about the largest Ponzi scheme ever in history involving "overseas private promissory notes". In 2017 registered broker dealers were involved in billions of dollars of fraudulent promissory note transactions in the US Securities market.

Why does this matter?

Everything I structured into the overseas Mining & Exploration Company was a "Promissory Note".

Great.

I had to deal with a general prejudice on Promissory Notes going overseas. What was more was I had to show paperwork on a failed investment. The failed investment looked oddly like something my group of investigators roasted broker dealers for less than 6 months ago.

What do you think the Securities & Exchange Commission did once they saw paperwork that carried similar components to the scams, they investigated one year before?

I'm not talking about the SEC's thoughts. I'm talking about the SEC's actions.

The SEC started sending out informational subpoenas.

The SEC sent an information subpoena to every company I appeared to be involved with. The regulators sent subpoenas to companies I didn't even raise money for, charge fees to or direct money into. It would later turn out the reason why they notified so many people was because the regulators literally read every single one of my emails. I used my financial advisor email to write things that had nothing to do with clients, client money, or even financial advisor business. I treated it as my personal email with the thought, "As long as I have a good legal disclaimer and don't do contracts through this email it doesn't matter". That's perfect to avoid a lawsuit. That does not avoid a nosey regulator whose only job is to "find something wrong". In my inexperience to appreciate how a routine checkup goes for registered investment advisors I lacked knowledge on basic separation of business. This knowledge I hoped would come from my more experienced partners, but it didn't. My +10 years partners never addressed the fact I should not talk about unrelated stuff through my work email.

I felt like Hillary Clinton with her Gmail server.

Now people who had nothing to do with anything I did were having regulators ask them about stuff that they had no business knowing. I was literally watching regulators jump from cause to cause. When one they previously investigated yielded "nothing" they would move on to another. No one likes to waste their time. These investigators were "determined" to find something.

My vendor for hot dogs need not know that I have client money in a biotechnology company. More importantly, my vendor for hot dogs need not be pressed if they invested any money into the biotechnology. Worse my vendor for hot dogs need not be grilled for 3 hours on how much they know about me.

This stuff just looks bad.

What's worse is there is absolutely no reason for it. My hotdog vendor knows nothing and he is now standing around wondering if he should let me buy a hotdog.

What do you think the reaction is to a routine check to make sure that nothing is wrong?

How do you think someone reacts to a subpoena from the United States Department of Alcohol Tobacco and Firearms (ATF) on weapons distribution money given in a compliant way to your affiliate company partner? Even if the basis for the subpoena is for unrelated activities?

The person, especially if they have zero experience, would most likely freak out. Even though there is no liability from the original party it doesn't matter. The ATF has to investigate it. That is the ATF's job. The fact a regulated business gave money to someone requires a formal investigation. It requires a formal investigation even if a non related activity occurred where the person was found to be nonrelated. Also remember the government doesn't just call you up for a quick call. It's not like the ATF will ask your opinion casually.

They call it an investigation.

There is a formal process for everything in government.

I received no fines, no bars, and no revocation of licensing. On the cover page the subpoena stated the following

"The investigation is a non-public fact finding inquiry. We are trying to determine whether there have been any violations of the federal securities laws. **The investigation does not mean we have concluded that anyone has violated the law. Also, the investigation does not mean that we have a negative opinion of any person, entity, or security.**"

Guess what everyone did that didn't understand it and care to read?

Panic.

The CEO of the biotechnology company had zero experience in anything business or securities related. Dr. C completely collapsed. It was like watching jelly try to hold its composure in the middle of 120 degree Celsius weather. Dr C instantly melted.

In business I made several faulty decisions. Being a **Businessman / Businesswoman** is not about identifying the proper gaps in the market. Being a **Businessman / Businesswoman** is not about disrupting an establishment. Being a **Businessman / Businesswoman** is not about creating something brand new.

Being a **Businessman / Businesswoman** is about making the proper decisions in a format that forecasts potential business liability. Once the liability is assessed we make a collective decision. If we cannot transfer the risk we do certain risk mitigations to ensure that the company does not fall apart when the risk occurs. An example of how I could have avoided a bad gold transaction would have been requiring an Indemnity Bond on the loan money. As a creditor I could have stipulated this as part of closing. I could have required the deductible to be escrowed with my attorney and then collected on the policy when bad news was given.

As a **Businessman** I could have also required Hustler J to make me a certificate holder on some form of Errors & Omission (E&O) Insurance. I could have made Hustler J give me a Statement of Work (SOW) and hold him accountable to milestones. If Hustler J lacked E&O, I could have refused his services.

In my error to make proper business decisions I created a hard situation for my lack of experience in business.

I never lacked Prudence as a **Professional Hustler**. What I lacked was "experience" in real "business". I had experience in "deals" where I "capitalized" in.

The two experiences are different.

I am sharing this story for you to understand how a misconceived notion of your achievements can create a delusion you are qualified to be a "Head Coach" in an unrelated game. It's like a "Safety" in football never calling an "Offensive Play". The "Safety" thinks he knows how to call an audible because of his personal statistics. The "Safety" thinks this because he leads the league in interceptions. Your ability to do one thing right doesn't entitle you to understand the whole component of an offensive play.

Once my former CEO melted for no real threat the support around me began to unwind. I watched Dr. C get hustled out of $20,000 in legal fees when I told him what he was going through was routine. I told Dr. C a good attorney would spend 8 hours at the subpoena to guide him through it at $300 USD an hour. We would have to pay for the attorneys travel and hotel. This would at most cost the company $5,000 from my experience. Dr. C didn't listen to my advice. Dr. C went to some legal attorneys I knew needed money. One attorney had lost his major client and another was going through a hard personal situation. I told Dr. C these attorneys were bias. Although they were both "right" about the "worst" possible outcome I told Dr. C it was unlikely. I tried to encourage patience or at worst-case scenario a 2nd opinion. Dr. C didn't want a second opinion. Dr. C wanted to get out of what he thought was hot water. I watched Dr. C get advised by parties I knew were "hurting" for money. These parties preyed upon Dr. C's fear until he ended up losing 15 lbs in the process. This fear caused a full-blown panic in Dr. C's significant other. Dr. C asked me to resign due to personal advice given by the lead vulture and pressure from his wife. Then I told Dr. C if I resigned that vultures would consume him. I told this to Dr. C because no one had any stake in it. The people would squeeze every last dollar out of the account because of his "improper" assessment of the "situation". I also told him if I resigned and left so abruptly the $1,500,000 in investment would not come in. I didn't say this because I was threatening Dr. C. I made this statement because I understood each person intimately. I was the *Hustler* who made the people believe in the company. Belief in our company came through my sister's story, the passion I had for success, and the obvious genuine sentiments I held. I had the drive to succeed. I would tear up whenever I told my sister's story. I spent days with these people. I smoked cigars with them. I developed a very personal relationship. These people connected with me and were prepared to invest in a person like that.

That wasn't an act.

That was real.

People saw that.

Dr. C had none of that.

Dr. C didn't have a life to literally fight for. I made people believe their money would go to good deeds. I had my family to fight for. People wanted to help someone like that out. I didn't impress them with my "business". I impressed people with my real life story. Dr. C had no real life story. Dr. C could not make someone emotionally motivated to save one of his personal siblings' lives. Dr. C had to stand on his own two feet. What can one reference that hasn't gone the distance in business really say about a leader? What can one foot in one foot out say about a person? I did the company "full-time" while Dr. C did his thing back home 50% of the time. I closed my practice. I didn't have a way of earning income anymore. I was fully committed to the company I incorporated. Dr. C didn't burn his ship on an island and say there was no way off. Dr. C wasn't fully committed. Dr. C on multiple times told me he "needed" at least 3mm in his personal account before he would step away from his full-time job. Guess who was tasked with making his 3mm happen? You guessed right.

Me.

I burned my escape down when I closed my practice.

I saw no reason to keep the focus on a company I believed destined for greatness. I had enough in place where even if all the investment pulled out the USDA was obligated to continue the CRADA. All that would happen (at worst case) was the company would take a side step to a larger partner. The USDA would find a properly capitalized commercial partner (most likely a Monsanto) if the company could not make its second milestone payment. The lion's share would go to the new partner but the company would always receive a perpetual royalty. It wasn't about "winning", it was about "how much you win".

I resigned quietly.

Everything I predicted happened...happened. Dr. C was preyed upon for all the money in the company. Dr. C evaporated nearly $50,000 in cash on false pretenses only to find out "the regulators edified my view." The whole thing was punted as not really that urgent by the lead SEC Attorney. It would not be until nearly 3 years later I would have my civil suit filed for alleged insufficient disclosures and when I declined their offer to settle an indictment. The vulture attorneys made a comment that "it was better safe than sorry". Through the grape vine I heard that once the SEC investigation was over I could come back. The issue is – Dr. C burnt through all the money. Dr. C also made me sign a letter that said I could no longer represent the company. Dr. C was left without anyone in his corner except the one man that I brought on board. Dr. C single handedly made a decision that shook investor confidence and made 1.5mm withdraw in support. Dr. C unwound 8 months of work in 7 days of fear. The person that would come to be the new CEO saw this coming and realized what was happening. I am grateful for him keeping his integrity and being "honorable".

That was something the decision makers lacked.

The main investor in California backed out despite when this was happening we fully disclosed it. I flew with Dr. C and my close friend to disclose all the items surrounding my subpoena to him. His response was to make a joke and talk about how regulators were "too weak to be anyone so they preyed upon people who had the audacity to try".

The main investor gave us his full support. He actually told us I could stay in his guest house if the heat got too hot. Imagine that?

Do you know why our main investor pulled out from giving more money?

No one consulted him on ousting me from the company. More importantly, the investor did not agree with the decision. The main investor lost confidence in the company because the CEO lacked leadership abilities and prudent decision-making skills in business. The investor saw that the CEO was a product of fear. Dr. C could not take any struggle or hardship in business. I know this not because this was my opinion about the situation. I know this because the investor is still one of my main supporters after this situation. I know this because he said "If there is anything I can do to help...let me know". I know this because those were the words that came out of his mouth.

I saw the leadership changeover coming before it happened. I was happy when it came. I knew my former CEO could not make a good business decision. He had taken the soul out of the company. The soul was my passion, my tears for my sister, and the genuine drive I had to make it work at all costs.

It became further edified when the only thing Dr. C did was claim he understood nothing throughout the whole process. I do not know about you – but if you read how I write...I talk the same way. Also...claiming incompetence is at best "negligent" when you are the leader of a company.

I write and speak in something called third-grade language.

What really happened to my former CEO was the fear of losing his academic career to "earn" money as an *"Employee"*. A "Save yourself Syndrome" fear overcame Dr. C. Combined with the fact that Dr. C was losing weight at incredible rates in front of his new wife it was a recipe for disaster. Dr. C's new wife panicked as if their entire livelihood was about to be lost. Who could blame her? She had never seen Dr. C like this in their relationship. Was she walking into the end of his career? Was she walking into him being prosecuted? She had no idea. Dr. C had no idea. Dr. C's fear compounded her fear. Desperate attorneys looking to make money before the holidays exploited this. Dr. C magnified bad emotions and was completely taken advantage of.

Remember this statement, **"The investigation does not mean we have concluded that anyone has violated the law. Also, the investigation does not mean that we have a negative opinion of any person, entity, or security."**

No one paid attention to that on Dr. C's side. If Dr. C would have just taken a strong stance and said, "This man is in the middle of getting our company transferred 1.5mm USD. He negotiated it. He met the investors and he did this all by himself. He has raised every single dime that has come into this company. He disclosed it up front to our 1mm investor and the guy didn't even blink an eye. Our main guy gave us his confirmation of support. He put more money than all of us by a multiple of more than 100. No one knows me and our overseas people in Vietnam have never even met me. The money going into our separate Vietnam venture will crumble if the lead guy disappears in the middle of a pending transfer. I know science not raising capital. I'm smart enough to know that I can't come in the middle of a deal by saying they booted out the guy that convinced you to invest because of a routine SEC inquiry from his old practice. He has to be the one to bring it to a close. There is no formal order, fine, or proceeding against him. I hear what everyone is saying but you know what? This could all blow over and everyone would have just over reacted. I will not overreact. I'm deciding to wait to see if someone tells me officially he has a violation. If he did something wrong, I will terminate him without need for resignation. I don't have to ask him to resign if he broke a securities law. I can fire him. If he didn't, then we are not talking about anything."

Did Dr. C have enough backbone to stand up and fight for me?

Nope.

Dr. C was too busy worrying about keeping his job so he ran from his post as CEO.

You need to be careful of three types of people in any deal you get involved in.

1. Don't Know
2. Don't Care
3. Don't Understand

Dr. C and his newlywed wife had the perfect combination of these characteristics. The newlywed wife could care less about a magical 100mm USD in 24 months. This was a woman watching her husband lose weight at an unhealthy rate. The CEO was now claiming "He understood nothing" and caught several times saying, "He didn't know". All the "Didn't Know" turned into "Oh I forgot." My close friend would get so upset at him he would later resign due to what he thought was deliberate lies to unfairly dump all the responsibility on me. I will assume the best on those ones. My former partners in the financial advisor did the same things despite being 10 to 30 years my senior once they were pulled into the biotechnology issues.

Of course, a 33-year old with 3 year history as a Series 65 duped a 15-year veteran and a 40-year veteran PhD on tax, securities law, and corporate law. That makes a lot of sense. *Especially when the 33-year old introduced himself as someone being mentored by his partners.* The team solicited every person (not me directly) in an effort to pay themselves. Ironically, the team would be paid more than the person they claimed was at fault.

In my error to scale "opportunity" to "business" I created a situation where I lost my position.

I created a hard situation for an inexperienced CEO. I made bad decisions to blunder through the Bermuda endeavor. I tried to make up my mistake with an unrelated venture.

I would have probably been able to fight for my spot in the company if the company hadn't taken the loss in the overseas investment.

If this book was centered on being a "**Businessman**" this would be a lesson on "failure". I would categorize this as a failure because they pushed me out of a business I founded. People who had no money at stake pushed me out of the business (save for Dr. C's $15,000). This book would be about how I foolishly closed a successful practice to pursue something that would cause my bankruptcy.

I would have to file bankruptcy because I constantly took my earnings and gave it towards businesses that would reciprocate nothing back towards me. Remember what I said about **Professional Entrepreneur** team members? Do you recall Red Teams?

The failure of my ability to identify proper business partners means I created a false loyalty. No one came to my defense except my brother and close friend. Everyone else abandoned me. My brother had no directorship position and my close friend was one person with a directorship position. There was only so much they both could do with someone who held 90% of all proxy votes.

Partners or employees of entrepreneurial endeavors that scale into a business are staffed by mavericks. Mavericks are people who will typically hold out their hands with a **Professional Entrepreneur.** Their hands are held out based on deserving "talents". Mavericks deserve to get paid because they perform. Mavericks behave like Terrell Owens or Allen Iverson. If you do not know who those sports people are, look them up. Those people are talented individuals who have a hard time playing nice. When no one "procures" money except the **Professional Entrepreneur** everyone will leave when the money dries up.

Once I could not bring in the money everyone left.

I do not want you to think for one second that as a **Professional Entrepreneur** you cannot find people who will be loyal or support you.

I do not want you to think this is a great bash on Dr. C for failing to stand up for me.

That is not what this book is about nor am I saying that.

What I am teaching in this lesson is that exceptional **Professional Hustlers** are vital to a "team". If an entrepreneurial endeavor will change into a "business" there must be a seasoned business person involved. I recruited a bunch of mavericks who I could lead – but they were only being led while money was there. Wolves will not lead you to nothing. Wolves are hungry. Wolves are looking to eat. I also had no seasoned business people involved in the biotechnology company. The icing on the cake was no one put a sizable investment into the start up beside me.

As a result, I gave all the power to the most inexperienced and ill-qualified people to make "experienced" decisions. How do I know this is true? The CEO resigned within a month of my resignation to a research role and the company is being run by someone else.

These statements are not my opinion. I base the statements on observations of what happened. The new CEO will pick up my phone call and text me back usually within a few hours.

What about the old CEO?

The old CEO will not even thank me for saying happy birthday to him.

Let's ask some hard questions about my actions. Let's be fair. Because of my actions let's answer these questions:

Did the old CEO get fined?

Did the old CEO get sued?

Did the old CEO lose their job?

Did the old CEO get divorced?

Did the old CEO get sanctioned?

Did the old CEO get barred from participating on an offering?

Did the old CEO get voted out of office?

Did the shareholders incite some revolt against the old CEO?

The answer to these questions is a flat out "No."

What happened within 30 days of my departure? A new CEO took over and had 1mm committed to the company within this period. Exactly what I told Dr. C would happen...happened.

I told Dr. C that the money would still come in. There was nothing wrong with the company and if the SEC dug into the company they would uncover a gem. We were in partnership with a US Government Agency to do real research work. We allocated 95% of the money to legitimate business items.

The one questionable item was a bad decision to earn money for the company. There is no crime for a bad decision that is legitimately trying to benefit the company. There is only an issue if there is a failure to disclose.

Everyone had bullet-proof contracts and great signed conflict of interest letters in plain English.

We were fine.

Dr. C as the former CEO lacked the experience to judge the situation, assess what was happening, and determine a proper plan of action because of his inexperience. The best thing the old CEO did was resign. The worst thing I ever did was to empower someone who had less experience than me. That shows the novice nature in business I had. Now I am not a novice in this respect.

Too little too late?

I don't think so.

Frequently **Businessmen** and **Businesswomen** have different cultures than **Professional Entrepreneurs**. The **Professional Entrepreneur** *can clash* with a good **Businessperson**. **Professional Entrepreneurs** usually obsess over quick movement, taking advantage of an opportunity, and operate under very tight windows to "capitalize".

Businessmen and **Businesswomen** build "brands" that are long termed.

The term of a **Professional Hustler** is limited by their opportunity. Because of the limited scope to a **Professional Hustler's** endeavor, the people who flock to them are others like them. Never forget that everything is usually unique in an entrepreneurial endeavor. I am not mad with any of my former mavericks of the financial advisor or Dr. C. I am disappointed in them for not trying to bring me another opportunity. I am disappointed that I placed Dr. C in a position he was not prepared for. That is true. I am not mad at them, nor do I harbor ill will.

The uniqueness of the endeavor is an advantage. The unique nature of this advantage can backfire. The backfire in an entrepreneurial endeavor is usually caused by no one having experience. When no one has experience, there can be a limit to what others contribute to the bottom line in a **Professional Entrepreneur's** endeavor.

Often the greatest value can also be the greatest hindrance.

My final year I grossed over 500,000. All I had to do was "stay in my lane". At the rate my entrepreneurial endeavors were growing my actions would have clipped 600,000 before the year was out (stopped in August 2018). I probably would have clipped 750,000 the following year. Do you remember the analogy I gave you about Titans challenging the Greek gods?

In my zealous hubris I wielded my hammer at the heavens and demanded that Zeus descend to face the "Wrath of Thor".

Thor is not in the same league as Zeus.

Thor is not even Greek. Thor is from the Norse legends. This story is a complete mix up. That is the point. Thor is not part of Greece. Thor should not be carrying on in the legends of the Greeks. More importantly, Thor is not even a Titan. If Thor is anything, Thor is a Demi-god.

Are you following my point here?

I confused my identity and entered a realm I had no understanding of. As a result, I lacked certain foresight to anticipate likely events to my business. As a result I failed as a "**Businessman**".

This is an important lesson.

There is a more important lesson I have learned from this. If my life-long dream was to continue to grow as a "**Businessman**" this would be a very important part of my journey. I probably would not tell you about this journey for another few years. After all every journey has to end somewhere right?

That is not the point of my life or this book. The point of my life is to remember what I have worked so hard at. I have worked to be original. I have worked to be like no one else. I have worked to lead Red Teams. I love project management because one day whatever I am doing is finished. I do not like doing the same thing over and over. I want new challenges, new ideas, new careers, and new beginnings.

As a result my "*profession*" is perfect. My "*profession*" is a **Professional Hustler.**

No matter how the biotechnology company finishes its business cycle the endeavor will be one of my top 5 gross earning opportunities. My real estate and mortgage company will always top anything I previously did. It is aggressive to earn 7 figures for anything entrepreneurial based that develops "zero brand".

My family estate still has a sizable equity stake. Should my family benefit from my efforts it will be great.

If not.

I am a **Professional Hustler.**

I have another year to do what I always do.

I will earn more than any other *profession.*

Then I Didn't

I<small>F YOU GO</small> online and research the question, "What is the difference between an Entrepreneur and a Businessman?" it will surprise you. No one agrees on what the answer is. Let's take a quick look of what some people say. I will literally go by the Google search engine results on 23 February 2019 at 354PM CST to see what the public thinks. This is not meant to be an authority just to see what Google indexes.

According to the number 1 search result which is an article published on "keydifferences.com" dated September 7th 2015, by Surbhi S:

"A businessman walks on the defined path, but an entrepreneur believes in making his own path, which becomes a guideline for other businessmen. Most of the people have a misconception that the terms businessman and entrepreneur, carry the same meaning, due to which they use them interchangeably."

Okay at least this one says there is a difference. I don't know about an Entrepreneur being a guideline for businessmen. All you have to do is read the previous chapter.

Number 2 is something from "Authority Website Income" from a writer named *Jon Gillham*. Gillham published something called "10 Differences between a Businessman and Entrepreneur" on February, 1 2015. According to John

"A businessman can make a business out of an unoriginal business or product idea. He enters existing businesses, such as franchising and retailing. He chooses a hot and profitable business idea regardless of whether it is his original idea or borrowed from someone else."

Not too bad. What does John continue to say?

"An entrepreneur is an inventor and the first creator of a product. He invests time, energy and money on his own idea. He doesn't start a business from an unoriginal idea. That is why he starts on a startup while a business-man starts on a business."

I wouldn't totally disagree with that but I would argue unoriginal ideas can be the safest opportunity. Remember *Personal Reasons*? Never forget about *Disorganization* either. Both are key components for a **Professional Entrepreneur** to capitalize.

I would say John is looking at the glass partial. John is only looking at the *Emerging Concept*.

Let's continue on to something that at least has a good name behind it like Forbes. Forbes is number 4. This answer comes from Peter Lynch, a VP at a Private Equity Firm. At least we can get something from someone putting money into a deal. Peter says the following based on spending more than a decade around Entrepreneurs (as opposed to researching it like our other two):

"Most entrepreneurial success stories do not rely on a new concept. Improving on an existing product would suffice."

That's interesting. He doesn't agree at all with what the other two said.

According to Peter the only difference is "The ability to persist when no one's watching for an extended duration."

Okay so according to Peter anyone who can persist at doing some-thing when no one is watching is an entrepreneur. In that case my youngest brother who will shoot a basketball for 4 hours when no one is looking is an entrepreneur. Mind you, I did not get to that point until I read half-way through the article. They published the post on November 15th 2016 under the title "There's a Subtle Difference Between a Businessman and an Entrepreneur".

I can keep going down the list.

Do you see what the issue is?

No one agrees what an Entrepreneur is. Do you know why no one knows what an entrepreneur is?

No one knows because the people trying to advise the general pub-lic do not choose their profession as a **Professional Entrepreneur**. The fact that the information available is from people who do "other things" means confusion is created. People who do not choose this path to sustain their entire livelihood can never understand what it is to be a **Professional Entrepreneur.**

You cannot meet a thousand entrepreneurs and then say, "I understand what it is to be an entrepreneur."

You must live it.

You must breathe it.

You must feel the pressure to perform.

You must be obligated to find revenue when there is none.

You must understand what it is like to survive solely on your ability to put together an opportunity.

If you have not done that you do not understand.

Let's see if we can find any government authority on what it is to be an *Entrepreneur*. The only US authority I could locate that cared to use the word was the Small Business Administration (SBA). The SBA has something called the "Office of Entrepreneurial Development". The current Associate Administrator is someone called Allen Gutierrez. The current Deputy Associate Administrator is Adriana Menchaca-Gendron (as of February 2019).

Do you know what the Deputy Associate Administrator's highlight was? I'll write it down for you.

"Prior to joining SBA, Adriana was the Deputy Executive Officer for the Office of Regulatory Affairs at the Food and Drug Administration (FDA), where she had oversight of a geographically dispersed organization with 220 employees and a budget of approximately $1 billion, providing support to over 4,500 regulatory employees. As the Deputy Executive Officer, Adriana led the areas of workforce development, human resources, management operations, budget, and financial management. Prior to joining FDA, Adriana was the Acting Deputy Chief Officer for Legislative, Regulatory and Intergovernmental Affairs in the Veterans Health Administration at the Department of Veterans Affairs. Adriana has also worked in the Office of the Inspector General and the Office of the Chief Financial Officer at the Department of Labor."

According to the government the most qualified person to judge what an *Entrepreneur* is was a person who spent her time in a regulatory agency managing a tax payer budget of 1 billion.

What about our Associate Administrator? What was his background? Can we locate any large business deal that created some monumental feat innovating something in an emerging market?

"…Gutierrez served as the national executive director of The Latino Coalition (TLC). Under his leadership, the coalition grew to include 1.2 million Hispanic business owners and over 90 coalition partners, transforming TLC into one of the nation's largest and most effective Latino advocacy groups."

Okay so basically Gutierrez managed a political action committee to push Hispanic members' agendas. Basically Gutierrez at best <u>met some entrepreneurs</u>.

I scoured the SBA website for a formal definition. Do you know what my search returned?

Nothing.

So we have the top 3 Google search engine results returning conflicting information and a government led office that does not define the term. More importantly the leader is someone who spent her time at the FDA approving drugs and managing government employees.

I am not taking anything away from anyone's career. Each person has their own accomplishments they should have pride in. The thing is…no one here is an *entrepreneur.*

Let's see if we can grab a quote on what it is to be an *entrepreneur* <u>from someone who made their net worth past 100mm</u>. Mr. Combs is known by one of my close friends in the entertainment industry so I like to cite him. Let's look at Mr. Sean Combs, Puff Daddy. Mr. Combs was born in Harlem on November 4th 1969. According to entrepreneur.com Combs started his entrepreneurship career with newspaper routes, talked his way into internship at Uptown Records, became an executive within Uptown and then launched his own record label in 1993. Mr. Combs found and produced numerous artists by locating them "before" discovery. Mr. Combs then launched his own album (despite not being a rapper), became an actor, launched a fashion line and is currently working on a cable music network.

Without getting into the details what do you notice about Mr. Combs?

Mr. Combs went through multiple industries depending on what the opportunity was. I want to take a quote from Mr. Combs as published on the article "From Paper Boy to Music Mogul: Entrepreneurship Lessons From Sean "Diddy" Combs:

"When you are in a business, you are really responsible -- especially if you have a staff -- you are responsible for your investment and you are responsible to the people that work for you and so sometimes you gotta make the hard decisions. Sometimes you gotta make more of the conservative decisions," says Combs. "But also, any true entrepreneur knows that at some point you have to make that gamble." (Sean Combs, Entreprenuer. com Article 10/4/2013 – Clifford, C. CNBC)

See what Combs says is something very important that entrepreneurs understand. Sometimes you exercise a <u>conservative decision</u> but the more important thing Combs says is something more. Mr. Combs says that **any true entrepreneur knows at some point you have to make that gamble**.

What was my gamble?

My gamble was recovering money lost in my biotechnology company by diversifying into a high risk gold investment. In one transaction I attempted to recover a loss that *Hustler J* had advised me into.

Remember all I talk about is +50% a year returns to justify my "Cost Benefit Analysis" right? Also remember my tendency is at best 7-5-1.

Now we understand how different a true entrepreneur thinks from pretenders let me ask you a question.

How do you think doubling your money sounds to a regulator?

What would it look like to a regulator who has never opened up their own business account?

What about my regulator, the SEC?

What do you think my regulator thought when my regulator saw my one failed overseas investment?

Notice I said "one" failed investment.

That's it.

I managed as much as 286mm USD in reported assets. Do you know what represented the loss ratio in this failed investment?

Only 1.1mm.

The SEC would later claim the number was 3.7mm (although I am still trying to figure out where that came from) and over 70 clients (even though I think at most I had 30). They would then say I misreported by assets under management because I didn't have trading authority over the accounts.

Do you know what portion of my assets was involved in speculative stuff? Do you know how much I allocated from the capital I raised in my biotechnology company? Let's review. I raised $3,676,228.65 of hard cash. Of that $100,000 of the number was my personal money or my family's estate money. From the biotechnology company I allocated a whopping $150,000. I chose to "gamble" 4.08% of the money I raised. Some could say it was my money depending on how you track each dollar.

I engaged in aggressive investments with less than 4% of my biotechnology's raised capital and less than 3% of my total portfolio.

That's it.

I had an active management in these types of asset classes of $4,280,668.65. I had between my "Assets Under Advisement" and "Assets Under Management" more than 286mm USD at one point. The Delinquency rate was approximately 2.7% with a default rate of 4.4% at the time of my closing. As a whole the portfolio managed in the alternative asset classes grew by 61.7%. The growth cash number was $2,641,172.56 at closing of my firm in this small asset class.

If we count the entire blunder of the overseas Mining & Exploration Company (due to fraud and theft which occurred post closing of my firm) of 1,056,000 I would still have overall growth. My overall growth would be $1,585,172.56. This is an overall return of 37.03% on the "entire portfolio".

On a macro-level I was doing good performance. I always earn more than I lose. The issue was some people that were involved in this managed portfolio had what's called "Concentration Risk".

A person who is concentrated has everything in a failed venture.

The paperwork I made stated in bold letters **"Do not invest more than 10% of your liquid net worth. Investing more than this amount is fundamentally unsuitable due to risk..."**

I believed a person who called himself my "Mentor" was guiding me to follow the rules of capital placement. I would pay a price for complacency. My "Mentor" was a person with a PhD in Tax law, Securities Experience, and 30 years in corporate tax returns. I did not believe he would put people who didn't belong into my opportunities. The people would sign documents testifying to something they were not. According to the **Saturated Market** standard for engaging in these types of opportunities we were way out of line. Apparently the 30 year veteran who owned a tax practice could not judge who was an "*Accredited Investor*". My partners' desire to make their "ten percent" overshadowed any obligation to verify the paperwork coming in that said "I am an Accredited Investor". My "Mentor" was running in the red on some movie and needed cash. So he began to pump people through my firm.

Guess who had the title of Chief Compliance Officer?

Yep…I did.

Guess what my "Mentor" wanted? The guy wanted me to give him money to fund his next payment on his movie. I gave him money every time he sent someone my way. To be compliant it would be to purchase his company. He also asked for $25,000 up front before we started this arrangement. I gave it to him. How much I gave him depended on what he sent my way.

In my own opinion, he committed securities fraud. I never received my ownership certificates and when I asked him to buyout my equity he disappeared. I had my series 65. You can't sign a contract that says you are selling me ownership, I pay hard cash for it, and then you not give it to me. That is textbook securities fraud.

I could have roasted the old man, but I figured he had a short time before he would have to answer for his actions. He already had one heart attack while we were in partnership. I didn't need to be the reason he ended up in the dirt. So I gave his fraud a pass. Hopefully, the world gives me a pass one day.

The fact a few "unaccredited investors" would get into a boat unnoticed by my watchman meant we had some stowaways.

When customs would board our ship, they would find people that didn't belong there.

All our paperwork was tight. Either these people lied to get in on the opportunity of a **Professional Hustler** or one of my Mavericks went rogue. I wasn't there when the paperwork was signed so I won't ever find out the answer. Each person will say the opposite. Who knows what happened in private? All I know is each one had a declaration saying they understood the risks, indemnified every person, and were "Accredited". Each person wanted a plus 10% a year return with a possible upside of 50% for doing the deal. That much I am certain.

Who doesn't?

You know what a regulator sees when an entrepreneurial endeavor goes south?

The regulator in their ignorance to understand what is happening tries to put someone's feet to the fire. When a person who had no business getting into this risk enters the fire the one who gets burned is you.

As far as a regulator is concerned the actions are fraud, deception, or negligence.

What do you think I ended up getting?

I was thrown in the boat of negligence and insufficient disclosure.

With all my attention being put on the biotechnology company, the Chief Compliance Officer (me) "failed to supervise". More importantly, the Chief Compliance Officer made "clerical" errors on their application to the Securities & Exchange Commission. The Chief Compliance Officer in his infinite wisdom figured he could pay a third party to handle paperwork he was responsible for. Not a smart move. Don't ever pay someone to do something they are not responsible for.

Folks let's be clear about something in highly regulated **Saturated Markets.**

If you don't have the experience or patience to be mentored in a top firm, do not enter the market.

Do not assume a title you are not qualified for. Do not put your faith in mavericks that have 20 years experience.

At the end of the day people will try to dump things on you regardless of what the truth is. All parties will plead ignorance.

The sound of my name was now the sound of a potential subpoena for unwanted inquires. My relationships were at best "burnt out". Others were just "tired" of hearing the regulators make verbal claims with no hard proof. Some were "stressed out" and just stopped picking up the phone.

I received exactly "zero" law-suits from these events (as of the time of my writing) from any individual.

I did receive a government indictment on wire fraud, a civil suit from the SEC on disgorgement (ill-gotten gains is the official term) and the SEC's opinion I made insufficient disclosures. Apparently, I was in this all for about 90k over three years and telling people I made money (but no exactly how much) from their investment wasn't enough. The wire fraud charges I am still dealing with. They correlate to sending money overseas on the failed gold investment which total just south of 1 million dollars.

I am the only one within reach. So it is easier I guess to go after me then the people who received the money.

The heat was too high and now the best I could get was "Chris let's wait for it to all blow over. Once this finishes we will get back together. For now, just take care of your family."

This is the death sentence for a **Professional Hustler** who thrives on interpersonal relationships. My lifeline was cut. They drained the blood that coursed through my career body. They defeated me.

I watched as person after person would call me up after the SEC inquiry. The response was the same.

"I stuck up for you man. I told them I didn't know what you did but the person I know doesn't sound like anything you're describing."

I heard variations of that story at least 7 times. That was only for people who talked with the SEC panel.

Some were just issued informational requests for documents. Those were easier to handle but it still resulted in the same old "Chris let's wait until it all blows over."

So what do you think happened to someone like me?

Was I done?

Was I washed up?

How do you think this story ends?

That depends on what you think is the end. Remember, a **Professional Hustler** always has a definitive start and a definitive end. The "deal" is always "temporary". Remember, I have always said a **Professional Hustler** is more like a Project Manager.

So what is the definition of a project again?

Project – a temporary endeavor undertaken to accomplish a specific goal with a definitive start and end.

I had my start and end as a financial advisor.

I had my start and end as an executive in a biotechnology firm

I had my start and end as a real estate investor.

I had my start and end on a lot of things.

So the real question I needed to ask myself was simple.

What is my next start?

Life Beyond Business

I STARTED THE pinnacle of my career with something simple. My crowning achievement set so many records. My crowning achievement occurred with a simple desire. My desire was a cliché thing. My desire was to "help". My desire was to "help" my sister out a life of suffering. This desire pushed me to do things never thought possible. I rooted my desire in the characteristic of "protection". I have always held a hidden fire for courage in the face of danger. This fire sparks when I feel I require it to "protect" someone else.

I use to say about my biotechnology company, "The only reason this business is working is because it started from the right place."

I said that to so many people. I was convinced that was true.

I'm still convinced it is true now. I am convinced my success going forward will be rooted in this conviction. As a **Professional Hustler** I have only one unanswered category.

I want to talk about characteristics necessary for truly helping others. With the right characteristics you can soar to new heights. Everyone thinks that conquering is the goal for a market. Everyone thinks monopolizing a market through hostility is required. I heard people say, "The Best Defense is a Good Offense."

I have witnessed overly aggressive fighters beat their competition to a pulp. In War warriors aggressively pursued outnumbered terrorists with something called "call for fires" (If you are not in the military look it up) to teach enemies' defeat.

I witnessed willpower of a person's desire to protect someone overcome their worst fears and limitations.

The Story of Boyle

"Oh God, do you see that?" his wife said.

Boyle saw it: the crumpled frame of a bike under the car's bumper, and tangled within it a boy, trapped. That's when Boyle got out and started running. For an agonizing eternity the Camaro screeched on, dragging the mass under it. As it slowed to a stop, he could hear the bicyclist pounding on the car with his free hand, screaming. Without hesitating Boyle bent down, grabbed the bottom of the chassis, and lifted with everything he had. Slowly, the car's frame rose a few inches. The bicyclist screamed for him to keep lifting. Boyle strained. "It's off me!" the boy yelled. Someone pulled him free, and Boyle let the car back down. (Psychology Today, Wise J., 10/4/2010)

That was a real story. The world record for dead-lifting a barbell is 1,003 pounds. A stock camaro weighs 3000 pounds. So how did Boyle pull off this incredible feat?

Human beings have two basic kinds of physical ability. The first ability is gross-motor skills involving large muscles. I consider activities such as running, punching, and jumping large muscle skills. Fine-motor skills involve small muscles. An example of utilizing small muscles would be threading a needle, writing, or putting a key in a lock. Fine motor skills decline quickly when we're under pressure. Gross-motor skills peak much later. A good analogy of when the brain recognizes that it should accelerate your skills is when a bear is nipping at your heels. You will run faster than you would normally run. For a mother it might be seeing her baby under a burning log.

Penn State Kinesiologist Vladimir Zatsiorsky researched how stress affects the performance of weightlifters. Zatsiorsky found that most of us, if we try to lift a heavy object under ordinary circumstances, can only use about 65 percent of our muscles' maximum theoretical strength. Trained weightlifters can do a bit better, achieving about 80 percent. We possess an automatic control system. Our internal control system limits the amount of strain we can put on our body's machinery. They design the limit so that we don't injure ourselves unnecessarily.

As the situation becomes more critical, it may become worth risking some injury. The limit to our body's physical capabilities automatically lifts upwards in an extreme situation. Under the pressure of competition, Zatsiorsky a trained weightlifter can heft up to an additional 12 percent.

See aggressive tactics and conquerors show obvious signs of success. The person can take large swaths of land, get resources, and command an area quickly.

Do you know what a call to protect creates?

The call to protect makes you pass normalcy.

Passing normalcy makes you exceptional.

Being exceptional is what legends we hear about have. We hear about legends for thousands of years. Legends begin with ordinary people. Ordinary people change from generation to generation until they represent a divine aura that seems unreal.

Hemingway held a phrase that was inspired by the Greek Demigod Hercules.

"A man may be destroyed but not defeated."

If you are unfamiliar with the legend of Hercules let me give some background on it. Hercules is the Roman name for the Greek hero Herakles. Hercules was the son of Zeus, king of the gods, and the mortal woman Alcmene. Zeus in Greek legend was always chasing women. In one instance Zeus took on the form of Alcmene's husband, Amphitryon. After going through a transformation to Amphitryon Zeus visited Alcmene one night in her bed. As a result of their encounter Hercules was born. Hercules was a demigod with incredible strength and stamina. Hercules performed amazing feats. Some feats Hercules did included wrestling death and traveling twice to the underworld. Hercules' life was far from easy from the moment of his birth. Most time Hercules relationships with others were disastrous. This was because Hera, the wife of Zeus, knew that Hercules was her husband's illegitimate son. Hera's jealously created a desire to destroy Hercules. In fact, Hercules was born with the name Alcaeus. Hercules took the name Herakles, meaning "Glory of Hera" later. The name was meant to signify that Hercules would become famous through his difficulties with the goddess.

They portrayed Hercules as a super-powered mortal who suffered disappointments, had bad days and even bad years. There is an interesting aspect of Hercules' character that should resonate with you. Hercules' divine strength and abilities meant he did not have to willingly submit to any of the labors or punishments imposed upon him. Hercules chose to suffer his indignities to prove his strength.

Hercules chose to endure hardship to strengthen his resolve.

See without struggle there would be no character. Without character there would be no integrity. Without any of these characteristics I could not be a **Professional Hustler**.

Without any of these characteristics you cannot be a **Professional Entrepreneur**.

Without these characteristics we cannot be Hercules.

Hercules' famous Twelve Labors or his servitude to the queen Omphale was done willingly. Hercules inner strength and ability to endure hardships made Hercules an inspirational figure to the ancient people that heard his story. Hercules was a symbol of stability amid chaos, even if it was a chaos he himself had caused.

The situations created by the decisions I made in business would be my foundation to build my next chapter.

My next chapter is now.

My next chapter is to help you, the **Professional Entrepreneur**.

I want to "protect" your "identity". I want to show you that it is possible to struggle through your labors. The struggle you endure will build your character. I want to show you that your character will become the basis of your integrity.

Integrity will make you exceptional.

You can become the nameless hero who is a legend.

I know your face…even if no one else does.

You might not have twelve labors. Maybe you will just have four labors. Maybe another will have ten.

I had 13 labors.

Some labors resulted in me holding a laser-etched crystal as my victory trophy.

Some labors resulted in me remembering "A man may be destroyed but not defeated."

My last venture created a great potential upside monetarily but destroyed my financial reputation. Was I defeated? Was I going to tuck tale and run? Would I be someone forgotten and shamed? Would I be the man who would not have his name spoken? Would I be a cover under a shadow?

Would I be someone unimportant?

I will be important to someone. I will be important to guide the **Professional Entrepreneur** and **Professional Hustler** through their labors. I will be the voice of "consistency" that is not "confusing". I will "protect" the "identity".

There is a saying I appreciate from the Middle East.

"If something were to come from other than God, you would find much contradiction in it."

Do I sound like a contradiction? As a *Hustler* I have clearly identified that what we do is a *"profession"*. Does this seem contradictory to your life? Do you disagree?

If you are a **Professional Entrepreneur** how many deals have you done?

If you are a **Professional Entrepreneur** how many businesses have you incorporated and dissolved?

If you are a **Professional Entrepreneur** how many industries have you been involved in?

If you are a **Professional Entrepreneur** how many times has someone told another person they didn't understand what you do?

If you are a **Professional Entrepreneur** how many years have you earned more than $138,000 for the year?

If you are a **Professional Entrepreneur** how many times have you walked through Wal-Mart to hand someone your business card and the person have no idea what it is?

As a **Professional Entrepreneur** you are someone. You will come to know **Businessmen, Businesswomen,** *Hustlers* and **Employees.** Remember who you are. Remember the summary of this book. Remember, everything you do is a Project.

A Project is – is a temporary endeavor undertaken to accomplish a specific goal with a definitive start and end.

Your Project needs team members.

Your team members will fit into specialized situations.

Your situations will come up for Personal Reasons, Emerging Concepts or Disorganization.

You must incorporate all your entities for tax and legal reasons.

They will know the opportunities of your incorporated entity as the purpose of your Special Purpose Vehicle (SPV).

As a result of these situations you must lead highly specialized members in your SPV called a "Red Team".

Red Teams understand how to fit into an SPV concept very well.

Your Red Teams are led the same way as a Wolf Pack is led.

You are the Wolf Pack Leader.

You will trail your pack to let your pack find its way to "kill" your "game".

Once you have "killed" your "game" your "packs members" may trail off somewhere else.

So let's sum up what this book is drilling down to.

As a whole you are a **Professional Entrepreneur.**

The **Professional Entrepreneur** is the "leader" of a Red Team – a unit organized (as an SPV) for a highly specialized purpose (i.e. your opportunity) that requires the participation of team members (your wolf pack) whom you must lead (the Professional Entrepreneur) on a temporary endeavor (project) that has a definitive start and end (you closing your deal and getting paid) that surfaced because of certain conditions (disorganization, personal reasons or an emerging concept).

Go get them wolf.

Information Sources

The following sources of information were used in preparing the book:

1. My personal experiences in various companies where I held positions.

2. National, regional and local economic data were compiled and reviewed. The sources used include the World Trade Organization, Summers, Larry (1991). "Regionalism and the World Trading System.", METI (2005). White Paper on International Economy and Trade 2005, Tokyo, Freund, Caroline (2000a) "Different Paths to Free Trade: The Gains from Regionalism". Quarterly Journal of Economics 115:4, 1317-1341, and Low, Patrick (1993). Trading free: The GATT and US trade policy in conjunction with several peer review papers (PhD collegian accredited). The peer review papers are not included in part of this report.

3. I have reviewed domestic and foreign pharmaceutical data sources to factor my valuation of the biotechnology company. The sources used include: *The Pharmaceutical Research and Manufacturers of America* (PhRMA) (http://www.phrma.org), **Nature Medicine 10**, 26-27 *"Androgen receptor outwits prostate cancer drugs"*, John T Isaacs1 & William B Isaacs (2004), **Nature 482**, 116-119, *"Structures of cyto-chrome P450 17A1 with prostate cancer drugs abiraterone and TOK-001"*, Natash M. DeVore & Emily E. Scott (2012), **Science 21**, Vol. 328 No. 5981 pp. 1031-1035, *"Coadministration of a Tumor-Penetrating Peptide Enhances the Efficacy of Cancer Drugs"*, Kazuki N. Sugahara, Tambet Teesalu, Priya Prakash Karmali, Venkata Ramana

Kotamraju, Lilach Agemy, Daniel R. Greenwald, Erkki Ruoslahti, **Nature Biotechnology 28**, 917-924, "*Biopharmaceutical Benchmarks 2010*", Gary Walsh.

4. Research of comparative business sale transaction data has been performed with bias from the author. This included data compilation from the private company sale databases, and publicly traded company sale databases. The transactional data, however, is not included in this report. My central sources were primarily the United States Small Business Administration (SBA), SBA Office of Entrepreneurial Education, Statista.com, Forbes.com and US Department of Labor.

5. I have consulted the World Bank (2011). Doing Business 2011, UNCTAD (2010). World Investment Report, 2010. Geneva, Baldwin, Robert (1980). "The Economics of the GATT" in Issues in International Economics, edited by Peter Oppenheimer. Stocksfield, England and Boston: Oriel, for the cost of capital data. This data were used in estimating the appropriate discount and capitalization rates.

6. Business financial statements and tax records of the author's personal subject businesses over the past 10 years. The business financials had to be constructed based off of 1) historical money management that may include bias from the author, 2) the past performance of business ventures which the judgment of success will vary according to each individual person's analysis, and 3) the methodology in which the author deployed to judge financial performance may not conform to Generally Accepted Accounting Principles (GAAP) which is the standard measure for how to measure a business' profitability.

7. **The Seed Industry in U.S. Agriculture: An Exploration of Data and Information on Crop Seed Markets, Regulation, Industry Structure, and Research and Development**. By Jorge Fernandez-Cornejo, with contributions from Jonathan Keller, David Spielman, Mohinder Gill, John King, and Paul Heisey. Resource Economics Division, Economic Research Service, U.S. Department of Agriculture. Agriculture Information Bulletin Number 786.

8. **2018 Small Business Profile** – United States Small Business Administration (SBA), SBA Office of Advocacy, published January 1st 2019.

9. **Contemporary Research on Parenting**: The Case for Nature & Nurture. American Psychologist, 55(2), 218-232. Collins A., Maccoby E., Steinberg L., Hetherington E., Bornstein M.

10. **Universal Basic Income**: A Working Paper. United Nations Development Programme – UNDP China. Zeng Y., Guerriero M., Valancia Lopez E., Haverman P. July 2017.

11. **We the Plaintiffs**. ELocal.com/Lawyers. ELcal USA LLC. Sub source data for table: pacificresearch.org – Pacific Research Institute| bjs.ojp.usdoj.gov/content/pub/pdf/ttvlc01.pdf | bjs. ojp.usdoj.gov/content/pub/pdf/cbjtsc05.pdf

12. **Yes You Really Can Lift a Car off a Trapped Child**. The Science behind Seemingly Impossible Feats of Strength. Psychology Today. Wise J. November 4th 2010

13. **Google Search Engine**. "What is the difference between an Entrepreneur and a businessman". Key word search. Conducted 2/23/2019 357PM CST.

Made in the USA
Middletown, DE
18 March 2022

62709849R00126